JUN   2015

Mindfulness
in Action

Mindfulness
in Action

Making Friends with Yourself
through Meditation and
Everyday Awareness

Chögyam Trungpa

Compiled, arranged, and edited by
Carolyn Rose Gimian

SHAMBHALA
Boston & London
2015

Shambhala Publications, Inc.
Horticultural Hall
300 Massachusetts Avenue
Boston, Massachusetts 02115
www.shambhala.com

9 8 7 6 5 4 3 2 1

First Edition
Printed in the United States of America

∞ This edition is printed on acid-free paper that meets the
American National Standards Institute Z39.48 Standard.
♻ This book is printed on 30% postconsumer recycled paper.
For more information please visit www.shambhala.com.

Distributed in the United States by Penguin Random House LLC
and in Canada by Random House of Canada Ltd

Designed by James D. Skatges

Library of Congress Cataloging-in-Publication Data
Trungpa, Chögyam, 1939–1987, author.
Mindfulness in action: making friends with yourself through meditation and
everyday awareness/Chögyam Trungpa; edited by Carolyn Rose Gimian.—
First edition.
pages   cm
ISBN 978-1-61180-020-3 (hardcover)
1. Meditation—Buddhism. I. Gimian, Carolyn Rose. II. Title.
BQ5612.T77 2015
294.3'4435—dc23
2014023013

To the vast family of all those who practice and live mindfully

Contents

Part Two

FOUNDATIONS OF MINDFULNESS

Part Three

MINDFULNESS IN ACTION

Editor's Preface

Just when we think that life couldn't get any more disconnected or accelerated, another technology or another shift in
our worldview propels us even faster into the future. We often
feel that we can't keep up and we can't slow down—but we
know that we must find a way to connect. Paradoxically, we are
constantly connected through our devices and our social media, yet with all this interaction, many people report feeling
more lonely and alienated, lacking a sense of community. So we
need other ways to connect with ourselves and with the world.
We need connections that will ground us.

Many people have discovered that mindfulness offers them
a down-to-earth yet immediate way to connect with themselves. It is simple acceptance, described here as making friends
with yourself. It is, as well, a means to unlock creativity and
compassion. Meditation is a powerful technique for developing
mindfulness, which can help us discover a way of being that is
authentic, relaxed, and gentle. Meditation also offers a way of
reexperiencing and investigating our world, as well as providing

the means to develop greater awareness and to work with our emotions.

Mindfulness in Action: Making Friends with Yourself through Meditation and Everyday Awareness is, as the title suggests, a book about mindfulness and its application in the context of our whole life. The book focuses on the practice of meditation as a tool for developing mindfulness and explores how mindfulness and awareness influence our everyday life. It is a book for people who want to explore mindfulness through the practice of meditation and also apply meditative insight in their lives. It includes instructions for the practice of meditation, as well as an in-depth look into the principles of mindfulness.

Tens of thousands of us in the Western world now practice various forms of meditation and mindfulness regularly, as well as other contemplative mind-body disciplines. Mindfulness techniques are being effectively used in schools, hospitals, the military, and many workplaces. This book is not about the specific application of mindfulness to any one profession, problem, or sector of society. Rather, it's about the fundamental experience of mindfulness and awareness, which can be applied in many settings.

The technique of meditation that is offered here is unique but closely related to other approaches to mindfulness meditation. It is a form of meditation that stresses openness and engagement with our world. This technique for mindfulness meditation is compatible with other approaches in that it emphasizes a sense of presence, simplicity, and the development of peace. It is also about developing insight and clear seeing in one's practice and daily life. The author invites people to try his approach, but the insights offered in this book apply to whatever approach to mindfulness meditation you employ.

Part One of the book introduces the practice of meditation in some detail, connecting it with a sense of heart and with experiences of gentleness, clarity, a positive experience of aloneness, and the discovery of compassion. In Part Two, the author offers us further perspectives on the foundations of mindfulness, which are presented here as strategies for deepening and enlivening our practice of meditation as well as for linking practice with everyday experience. In Part Three there are additional meditation instructions that address working with the emotions, as well as a discussion of walking meditation and working with our awareness in group retreat situations. There is also an exploration of how meditation makes us less self-centered, enabling us to be more open and available to our world. The final chapters of the book focus on working with the emotions in practice and everyday life, as well as touching on the intriguing possibility of a mindful society.

The author, Chögyam Trungpa, was a meditation teacher, originally from Tibet, who in the 1960s, '70s, and '80s taught extensively in English in Great Britain, the United States, and Canada at a time when this was rare for Asian teachers. He introduced tens of thousands of people to meditation. I undertook the compilation and editing of the material for this book out of an inspiration that he shared with these thousands of others and with me: that mindfulness and meditation are the means to make friends with ourselves in a fundamental and transformative way, and they can lead to mindfulness in action throughout our entire life. They can deepen our understanding of ourselves, increase our ability to work with the challenges in our lives, and enable us to be kind to others.

Chögyam Trungpa taught in a profoundly heartfelt fashion that still resonates in our situation today. He allows us to see that meditation is a potent and inspiring discipline, yet that it is also simple, effective, and ordinary. He shows us that mindfulness and meditation are worthwhile disciplines and that they work. The practice of meditation works with us and on us, making us more available to ourselves and to others. The practice is demanding, it can be challenging, it shows us the truth of who we are, but that is all part of the beauty of human life.

There are hundreds of books today on mindfulness and

meditation. The early seeds that were planted by Chögyam Trungpa and other pioneers are truly flourishing in this era. *Mindfulness in Action: Making Friends with Yourself through Meditation and Everyday Awareness* joins these volumes as an impassioned offering to help us find a genuine and joyful path through the speed, the heartbreak, and the confusion of life.

I hope that readers will find something special in these pages and that this book will prove both helpful and inspirational. I know that the author would wish that his presentation of a full and complete approach to mindfulness will help and inspire people, now as much as ever.

CAROLYN ROSE GIMIAN
November 2013

A note on language: The practice of meditation is referred to here as the sitting practice of meditation, meditation (with no qualifiers), sitting practice, practice, and sitting. All refer to the same practice, which is explained in detail in the book.

Part One

Making Friends
with Yourself

1

Meditation: An Intimate Relationship with Ourselves

Meditation is one of the main tools we have to develop and practice mindfulness. It is a way to look at ourselves scientifically, so that we can see our psychological situation precisely. Meditation practice is not an exotic or out-of-reach approach. It is immediate and personal, and it involves an intimate relationship with ourselves. It is getting to know ourselves by examining our actual psychological process without being ashamed of it. We are often critical of ourselves to the point where we may become our own enemies. Meditation is a way of ending that quarrel by making friends with ourselves. Then we may find that we are not as bad as we thought or had been told we were. Before we look at other aspects of mindfulness, I'd like to give you some idea of the benefits of meditation, as they relate to our relationship with ourselves and our everyday life.

If we label ourselves as hopeless cases or see ourselves as villains, there is no way to use our own experience as a stepping-stone. If we take the attitude that there is something wrong with us, we must constantly look outside ourselves for something better than we are. That search can continue indefinitely, on and on and on.

In contrast to that approach, meditation is contacting our actual situation, the raw and rugged state of our mind and being. No matter what is there, we should look at it. It is similar to building a long-term friendship with someone. As part of the process of becoming friends, you get to know things that you do not like about someone, and you encounter parts of the relationship that are very uncomfortable. Acknowledging the problems and coming to terms with them is often the foundation for a long-term friendship. Having included those things from the beginning, you won't be shocked by them later on. Since you know all the negative aspects, you don't have to hide from that side of the relationship. Then you can cultivate the other side, the positive side, as well. That is also a very good way to start making friends with yourself. Otherwise, you might feel surprised and cheated later on, when you discover the things that you've been hiding from yourself.

Whatever exists in us is a natural situation. It is another dimension of natural beauty. People sometimes go to great lengths to appreciate nature, by climbing mountains, going on safari to see giraffes and lions in Africa, or taking a cruise to Antarctica. It is much simpler and more immediate to appreciate the natural beauty of ourselves. This is actually far more beautiful than exotic flora and fauna, far more fantastic, painful, colorful, and delightful.

Meditation is getting into this organic natural situation of what we are. It requires manual labor, individual effort, to do this. We can't rent a helicopter to fly us into the heart of the matter, without any inconvenience. We have to walk on our own feet. We have to walk into the countryside of this intimate natural beauty. That is the first step in developing mindfulness: going directly into our natural psychological situation without renting a fancy vehicle to get us there. We can't use an SUV or a helicopter. To begin with, we have to walk, which turns out to be worthwhile.

The practice of meditation presents us with straightforward techniques for the development of mindfulness that are valid for our actual psychological situation. We work with the resources that we already have. Our present situation, what we are, is our stepping-stone. We start with simple techniques such as sitting, walking, and breathing. These are natural things. We all have to breathe, we all have to sit down, and most of us can walk. These natural things are the starting point of developing mindfulness through the practice of meditation.

We have to start small, in an ordinary, simple way. In that sense, meditating is like collecting vegetables from your backyard rather than going to the supermarket to buy them. We just walk out into the garden and collect fresh vegetables and cook them. That is an analogy for the direct, personal, and immediate quality of meditation. It involves simplifying our basic psychology and our basic problems. Simplifying in this case means having no expectations about what you will gain by meditating. You just begin.

It might be best to think of developing mindfulness through meditation as a way of life rather than as a one-shot deal. To benefit from meditation you need more than a taste of it. You need to train yourself over a period of time. Otherwise there will be a lot of unnecessary confusion. So it's important to stick with the practice and follow the instructions that you receive.

The practice as it will be presented in this book is not necessarily more enlightening or promising than other techniques. However, if you stick with this approach and you apply exertion and patience, then regardless of your background or beliefs, you will have a chance to understand yourself better. I should warn you that such understanding might be extremely boring. Also, such understanding might include seeing some things you don't want to see. Nevertheless, we can't reject ourselves before we know who or what we are. So I encourage you to be brave.

Please don't chicken out. It won't help to reject yourself—or congratulate yourself. Rather, try to work simply with the technique as it's presented to you in the following chapters.

Meditation is extremely down to earth, irritatingly down to earth. It can also be demanding. If you stick with it, you will understand things about yourself and others, and you will gain clarity. If you practice regularly and follow this discipline, your experiences won't necessarily be dramatic, but you will have a sense of discovering yourself. Through the down-to-earth practice of meditation you can see the colors of your own existence. The earth begins to speak to you rather than heaven sending you messages, so to speak.

I personally learned something from this practice. This is not intended as a testimonial, but I want to share with you how I have benefited personally from the practice of meditation. In chapter 3 I will give you instruction in the technique of meditation as I learned it myself.

Meditation as I was taught it has several stages. The first stage is the development of basic mindfulness, which you can practice in a group or individually. At the beginning, this practice helps you to develop mindfulness by teaching you to pay attention to your breath, your ordinary breathing. When you're running around, you may get out of breath. Then, when you stop and sit down, the first thing you do is to try to regain your breath. At that point, you pay attention to your breathing. Or if you want to relax, you sit in a comfortable chair and say "Phew." So breathing is part of what we naturally associate with both exertion and relaxation. In chapter 3 we will talk specifically about how to work with your breath in the practice of meditation.

The technique of mindfulness meditation is associated with the development of peace. In fact, we might call it peaceful-living meditation. Peace here doesn't mean a state without war. It has nothing to do with politics. Here we are talking about peace as non-action. Say we are having an intense time with some situation in life, such as our relationship with a friend, with our parents, or with our business. When we step back from the intensity, we might also sit down and say "Phew!" Peace is that kind of flopping down. But please don't misunderstand what I'm saying. In the practice of meditation, you can't get this kind of peace without applying discipline and exertion.

Mindfulness is a specific and almost eccentric application of effort. It is like building a staircase. Making a set of stairs requires a precise measurement of the boards, so that the steps are built properly. All the angles must be carefully measured and cut, and the right nails must be used and hammered in precisely. The staircase has to bear the weight of people walking up it. We might ask: A staircase to what? At this point, the destination doesn't really matter. Just building the staircase is good, with no promise and no blame. Let us simplify the situation. Let us build this staircase very simply and directly. That is the essence of mindfulness.

Meditation can be a rather demanding process, but it is a very joyful situation, because we have the conviction that we are going to help ourselves by relying on our own effort and abilities. In that way, celebration is the heart of the practice of meditation.

When you begin to practice meditation, you may find yourself asking a lot of questions. You may ask yourself, "Is this going to work?" "Am I doing the technique correctly? Am I making mistakes?" As we continue to practice, we relax and go along with it more fully. Many of these concerns start to seem less relevant. The practice speaks for itself.

As time goes on, however, we may discover a whole new level of questioning. We may find ourselves creating elaborate intellectual, psychological, emotional, or sociological preoccupations for ourselves while we meditate. We find ourselves looking, questioning, lying back, analyzing, and trying to make sure. We will look at many of these responses and at how they can be worked with. However, you may also be encouraged to suspend those questions, especially when you are first learning the practice of meditation. When you suspend such concerns, your practice can be a simple statement that is direct and deliberate.

The basic point of mindfulness is this deliberateness. You are actually doing something. You are getting into the process, without needing to make sure that what you're doing is okay. We can discuss the philosophical and metaphysical aspects later on. For now, let us simply begin to make friends with ourselves.

2

Discovering Our
Capacity to Love

Before presenting the details of the technique of meditation practice and explaining how it leads to mindfulness—before we even begin to meditate—I'd like to look at our mentality. We often approach life as though we were defending ourselves from an attack. Many of us, when we were growing up, were frequently reprimanded in ways that made us feel bad about ourselves. Whether the criticism came from our parents, a teacher at school, or someone else, it tended to reinforce a feeling that there was something wrong with us. Criticism often produced a feeling of isolation, a feeling of *you* and *me,* separated by a great divide. We learned many defense mechanisms at an early age, thinking that a good defense would be the best protection from further reproach. We have continued this approach as adults. Whether it's a confrontation with a stranger on the street or an argument with our partner in the bedroom, we believe that we need good excuses to explain ourselves and good logic to defend ourselves. We behave almost as though we were professional negotiators, our own little lawyers.

In Western psychology, some approaches stress the importance of reinforcing ego to enhance self-esteem. We may misinterpret this to mean that we should promote ourselves at the expense of others. A person may become very self-centered with this attitude. It is like you are saying to the world, "Don't you know who I am? I am what I am. If I'm attacked for that, that's too bad. I'm on the side of the right." You feel justified in what you're doing, as if you had God on your side, or at least law and order on your side.

When we're first learning these techniques for self-defense, our logic may be somewhat feeble, but eventually we become powerful and convincing negotiators for ourselves. The whole process is based on one-upmanship. This sort of self-justification may be quite successful, but it is very aggressive.

We learn to apply this approach throughout much of our lives. We try to gain the upper hand with everyone, from university registrars to our boss at work. When we join an organization that collects dues, we might try to negotiate our way out of paying them. Maybe a few things are not negotiable, such as the price of a movie ticket, but if we don't like the movie, we'll try to get our money back. We try to negotiate everything in life to get the best deal for ourselves. It can become the basis for even our most intimate relationships: raising our children and dealing with our spouses, relatives, and friends.

Much of this goes back to our education and upbringing. We're still afraid that we'll be criticized or we'll fail if we don't assert ourselves. On some level we worry that we won't be functional if we aren't assertive. We might not be able to brush our teeth or comb our hair properly. We might never leave the house if we don't pump ourselves up.

Perhaps we should reexamine these assumptions, to see what really works. We need to investigate whether it's beneficial to build ourselves up, especially to do so by putting others down. We need to seriously question what is harmful and what is beneficial. In my own experience, I have found that employing a self-centered approach and being constantly on the defensive are not helpful.

Rather than reinforcing our "me-ness" and justifying ourselves constantly, we should base our lives on something more powerful and trustworthy. If we develop real trust in ourselves, constant self-defense is no longer required. That may sound good, but what are we going to trust in ourselves? To begin with, we need to conduct another examination. We need to look within ourselves. When we look, what do we see? Ask yourself: Is there something worthwhile and trustworthy in me? Of course there is! But it's so simple that we tend to miss it or discount it. When we look into ourselves we tend to fixate on our neurosis, restlessness, and aggression. Or we might fixate on how wonderful, accomplished, and invulnerable we are, but those feelings are usually superficial, covering up our insecurities. Take a look.

There is something else, something more than all that. We are *willing*: willing to wait, willing to smile, willing to be decent. We shouldn't discount that potential, that powerful seed of gentleness. Even the most vicious animals possess natural affection and gentleness for their young. That element of gentleness exists in every being. We don't have to be embarrassed about it or try to hide it. We don't need to cast ourselves as bad boys and girls or as heroines or tough guys. We can afford to acknowledge and cultivate gentleness and, first of all, to treat *ourselves* better. If we don't appreciate ourselves, we have no ground to work with ourselves.

The alternative is extending aggression, arrogance, and resentment—to our parents, our teachers, our relatives, our colleagues, our employees, our friends, and our lovers. The whole world seems full of thorns that cover the ground around us, and poisonous fumes are everywhere. Aggression is blind. Whenever there's a blind spot produced by your aggression, you don't see anything. Then, no appreciation or friendship is possible.

When you don't accept yourself, you often feel that you

have to lie and scheme in your self-defense. Once you start lying, you have to remember which lie you told to which person. But if you've told hundreds of lies, it takes a lot of energy to keep them straight, which puts a huge strain on you. It's neither effective nor maintainable in the long run. Eventually, you get caught in your own web of lies.

There is a much simpler way. If you decide to buy a shirt, you go to a store and pick one out on the basis of the cut, the fabric, the size, and the pattern. If the shirt fits, you generally feel good in it. Your new clothes feel clean and fresh. They don't come with dirt on them. Everything in life comes that way, without any need for logic to defend it. You might have trouble seeing this sometimes, but you yourself are also fine—excellent, in fact. Rather than deceiving other people and, more important, deceiving yourself, you can be as you are, which is more than good enough. It is worth appreciating ourselves, having affection for ourselves, and taking care of ourselves. Genuineness, goodness, and appreciation are extraordinary gifts. Ultimately, that is where we place our trust. This truth is so true that we don't have to pretend at all. It is real.

Every one of us is capable of loving ourselves. We are also capable of falling in love. We are capable of kissing our loved ones. We are capable of extending our arm to shake hands. We may offer a meal to someone, welcoming him or her to the table, saying, "Hello. How are you?" We are capable of these simple things. We've been performing such ordinary acts of kindness for a long time. Generally we don't make a big deal about this capability, but in some sense we should. We should celebrate or at least acknowledge our capacity for simple acts of generosity and gentleness. They are the real thing, and in the end they are much more powerful and transformative than aggression, egomania, and hatred.

When you appreciate yourself, you realize that you don't have to feel wretched or condemned. You don't have to artificially puff yourself up, either. You discover your basic dignity, which comes along with gentleness. You have always possessed this, but you may never have recognized it before. You don't have to be an egomaniac to appreciate yourself. In fact, you appreciate yourself more when you are free of the ugliness of that egotism, which is actually based on self-hatred.

Look in the mirror. Appreciate yourself. You look beautiful in a simple, humble way. When you choose your clothes, when you comb your hair, when you take a shower, you are expressing an element of complete and fundamental goodness, wakefulness, and decency. There is an alternative to feeling condemned. You actually can make friends with yourself.

This friendship with yourself is the basis, and the goal, of the practice of meditation. Meditation helps us to develop mindfulness and awareness, which allow us to gain another dimension of understanding ourselves. This makes us better friends to ourselves and to our world. Even before meditating, however, we can cultivate basic kindness toward ourselves. Without it, we have no way to move forward.

When I was first studying in Tibet, I sometimes thought that my tutors were trying to make me into a charlatan, a fake wise man, because what I was studying seemed divorced from my experience. However, when I received meditation instruction from my teacher and started to practice meditation myself, things began to make sense. I began to realize that there was something real that I could connect with. My experience and I myself were part of the teaching that I was receiving, rather than my only being taught something abstract from a book. Here, in this volume, I have tried to present an approach that reflects this understanding of the personal nature of meditation practice. I hope that you will have a similar experience in your own practice of meditation.

3

How to Meditate

If you are going to make bread, you need both flour and water for the dough. The practice of meditation is like the water, while your daily mindfulness and awareness, or your practice of mindfulness in action, is like the flour. To make the dough you combine the two. In this book, meditation is our starting point. Later on we will talk more about applying mindfulness in everyday life and about how meditation and the post-meditation situations work together.

Attitude

The basis for the practice of meditation is appreciation. Every breath we take is a gift, naturally pure and good. We appreciate every pebble in the riverbed, every apple on the tree. Ordinary activities are in themselves powerful and worth appreciating. From this point of view, there is no such thing as a contaminated or polluted situation. When we begin to view the world in this way, seeing every situation as part of a natural process, we bring this attitude to our practice of meditation. We see meditation as a process of natural evolution rather than seeing it as a highlight or something extraordinary.

We might say that the practice of meditation is a process of developing faith—not faith in something greater or beyond, but having faith in the immediate situation. We have faith and trust in the activity of meditation itself. Our approach is not frivolous at all. We are here to practice meditation, not to indulge ourselves.

Taking Your Seat

With that attitude you take your seat in meditation in an ordinary but deliberate way. As you approach your seat, you should feel that it's good, trustworthy. You should arrange your chair or your meditation cushion carefully. If the space has already been arranged for you, check to be sure that your chair or cushion is in the right spot and that you have what you need, including extra cushions or things of that nature. Then sit down and experience yourself sitting there. Every time you sit down to practice, it should begin in the same way, with an attitude of appreciation.

How you sit down and begin your practice is very telling. Sometimes when you go into a restaurant you storm through the door. There's a sign that says, "Seat yourself." You can sit wherever you like. You walk to your table with a garish swagger and sit down with a big plop. Hopefully, the chair or the booth doesn't collapse under you. You slump in your seat, and as you look at the menu, you blot out the world completely.

Taking your seat in meditation is quite different. You choose your spot with respect. You bend down gently to sit on your cushion or chair, keeping that sense of respect. As soon as you put your weight on the seat, you feel that good posture is possible, and almost automatically you are inspired to sit up straight.

When you are meditating, whether you are alone or sharing

the space with others, you always hold your seat properly. Then you feel that you are doing the practice with dignity. When you sit down to meditate, you are making a connection with the earth, whether you sit in a chair or on a cushion. It's almost as if a message is coming from the earth, encouraging you to hold your seat properly.

Posture

Posture is very important in the practice of meditation. This is equally true in everyday life, whether you are meditating or not. You may be driving a car, sitting in your living room, or reading a magazine in the dentist's waiting room. Your posture should always reflect an uplifted presence, wherever you take a seat.

Your posture in meditation can actually produce a psychological change in you. You begin to understand that your purpose is already accomplished, just by taking the posture of wakefulness. In a certain sense there's nothing more to do! You don't need a future goal. You can accomplish your goal on the spot, simply by sitting with good posture.

Posture in a Chair

When you practice meditation, you can sit in a chair or you can sit on a cushion on the floor. If you sit in a chair, your feet should touch the ground, or you should put a cushion under your feet. This provides a sense of touching the earth or being grounded, having some foundation for your posture. Also, if possible your knees should be slightly lower than your thighs. Depending on the chair, you may need to sit farther forward or you may need a cushion under part of your bottom. If you can, sit up straight so that your back is not leaning against the back of the chair. This will give you a more upright posture and will place less strain on your back and neck. It's also better not to use armrests unless absolutely necessary. You want your arms to be able to hang loosely from your shoulders.

Posture on a Cushion

When you sit on a meditation cushion, you cross your legs very simply. Your knees don't have to touch the ground, but it's helpful if they are at least slightly lower than your thighs. Otherwise, it causes a lot of strain on your lower back, and it's difficult to maintain an upright posture. If you find it difficult to lower your knees below the thighs, you probably need a higher cushion.

Once you have taken your seat and adjusted your legs, you straighten your back, not to the extreme but in a deliberate fashion. If you usually have a tendency to hunch over—which could give you a hunched outlook—in meditation you may find that you can straighten up. You sit well balanced in the middle of your seat, not leaning too far forward or back. You feel that you are sitting up straight, almost as though there were a thread attached to the top of your head, which tugs on your head if you aren't sitting up straight and encourages you to sit upright. At the same time, you have a slight concave curve in your lower spine, which helps you to have a solid base where your hips and buttocks touch the cushion. You relax your belly. Your shoulders and your neck are also relaxed but held beautifully in place, so that there is no strain. You tuck your chin in just a little bit.

The quality of your posture in meditation is similar to how you might hold yourself if you were going to ask someone to marry you. Your approach would be semi-relaxed, friendly, and slightly seductive, but also somewhat formal. That's how your posture should be here.

I've noticed that when people see something very interesting or exciting in a movie, they all sit up with perfect posture.

When the movie gets even slightly dull and uninteresting, people begin to slump and do all kinds of things with their hands and feet. But at first they have perfect posture. In meditation, we should feel like the moviegoer at the beginning of an engrossing scene. It is happening, it is your life, you are sitting up, and you are breathing. It is personal and direct. You are sitting upright, and with your head and shoulders you assume a dignified posture. Posture is extremely important.

Placing Your Hands

Whether you are sitting in a chair or on a meditation cushion on the ground, your hands should rest lightly but deliberately, palms down, on your thighs, a little bit above or just touching your knees. Placing your hands is a statement of deliberateness, and it, too, brings a feeling of dignity. This is sometimes called the mind-relaxing posture. Your hands are somewhat open—not clenched—and your fingers are not held tightly together. There's a little space between them. The tips of your fingers are a little ways back from the bend in your knees. You want your arms to be relaxed, not pulled forward nor held too close to your hips. You may have to experiment to find the right spot to place your hands.

Gaze

Your eyes are open, but you are looking somewhat down, about four to six feet in front of you. A traditional description is that you look ahead as if you were holding a plow yoked to a team of oxen.*

Your eyes might even be half-closed, so that they're relaxed, but it is not a spaced-out approach. You are just there, looking

---

* In this day and age, your eyes would be at a similar level as for pushing a Rototiller, a baby stroller, or a lawn mower.

ahead with an attitude that combines humility and positive pride, if you can imagine that.

Sometimes if you pay too much attention to visual details and colors, you develop tightness in your neck and a headache. In ordinary life we walk and move and look around quite a lot, so the whole process is balanced. In this case, you sit without moving around. Often there's not much noise, either, so everything is concentrated visually. This may result in visual tension, which can become a problem. The idea is not to focus too intently on the visual situation, but just to open your eyes without focusing too precisely on anything. Your gaze should be somewhat soft. In your practice you can experiment and discover for yourself what this means.

Mouth and Tongue

When I was at the dentist recently, she encouraged me not to grind my teeth and not to hold my jaw too tightly. She gave me a technique to help with this, which is to rest your tongue on the roof of your mouth. That coincides with the approach we take in meditation. The instructions for meditation encourage you to open your mouth slightly when you meditate, which helps you to relax. If you rest your tongue on the roof of your mouth, you can relax your whole face and jaw. You aren't clenching your jaw. The tip of the tongue is lightly placed on the roof of your mouth, just behind your teeth. That way your mouth is relaxed. Your mouth is slightly open, as though you were saying the syllable "ah."

Mindfulness of Breath

Once you establish your seat, all the aspects of your physical posture help you to focus your mind on the breath. Having a good seat and good posture almost automatically brings mindfulness of the breath.

The ground beneath you is solid and it supports you. Once you settle in your seat, the main thing that is happening is your breathing and a unified sense of your body and its systems all working together. Everything falls into place, into its *real* place. It feels so good. You find that you fit perfectly into the jigsaw puzzle of the awakened world. There is no struggle or artificiality involved. The situation feels good and precise— almost ideal.

Your breath is constantly going in and out. You can feel yourself inhaling and exhaling through your mouth and your nostrils. Just pay attention to your breath, your natural breath. It might be rough or deep if you had to run to get to the meditation hall. Or your breathing might be quite shallow. It doesn't really matter. Just feel your existing natural breathing. Sit quietly and listen to your breathing. To begin with, just listen to it. In that way you can settle down for a few minutes.

When you feel a little familiar with the breath, without straining too much, put your attention on the outbreath. Go out with the outbreath. Outbreath is an experience of the life force. In the Lamaze method of natural childbirth, they talk about breathing out and letting go as you are giving birth. This is a similar approach. The outbreath in meditation is like giving birth to the universe. You just let go.

You follow the outbreath very simply. Go along with it. Don't particularly try to feel the temperature of the breath in your nostrils or anything like that. Just breathe out, and as your breath goes out, you go out, very simply.

Then you are automatically willing to breathe in. You breathe out, and then you have a gap. Without extra effort, you will breath in naturally. When you look at a beautiful flower, you take in what you see, and then eventually you blink. That's like the gap at the end of the outbreath, which goes along with how you perceive your world. You project out, you perceive something, and then you give yourself a break: you blink. The break allows your brain to sort out and integrate your perceptions.* So the whole process is project, perceive, and take a break. That's how we experience our phenomenal world altogether.

Don't try to be too rigid and solemn about working with the breath. Keep everything simple and to the minimum. Working with the breath is a straightforward practice that is direct, real, and also revealing. You are simply being there.

Working with Thoughts

When you are in that space, holding your posture and following your breath, your mind will start to raise its own questions: "Now what?" "What does this mean? What does that mean?" When all those questions arise, you are reacting to hearing the sound of emptiness resounding in your mind. It is empty in the sense that there is no content in meditation. I'm not speaking literally about hearing a sound but about a reaction to slowing down and emptying out.

Your reaction, or the echo of emptiness, may take the form of anticipation, anxiety, or questioning. You are sitting without an object, without an agenda. You have nothing to do. Your mind begins to question what is going on because it's not used to the stillness. It will start to manufacture all kinds of entertainment.

You begin to realize that you have all sorts of thought patterns. What are you going to do about those? So many thoughts of past, present, and future will arise in your practice of medita-

---

* Chögyam Trungpa seemed to be anticipating modern developments with these comments on blinking. In January 2013, researchers at Osaka University in Japan reported findings that suggest that "blinking does more than stop our eyes drying out: it is an active process that causes the brain to go off-line, into a more reflective mode, before giving renewed attention." See Catharine Paddock, "Blinking Causes Brain to Go Off-Line," *MNT* (*Medical News Today*), January 3, 2013 (www.medicalnewstoday.com/articles/254543.php).

tion: thoughts about your life, your future plans, conversations with your friends and your relatives, all sorts of self-conscious gossip.

Let all these things come through. Let them just come through. Don't try to say whether they are bad or for that matter whether they are particularly good. Just let them come through, as simply as you can. That approach brings a sense of openness. You don't find your thoughts threatening or particularly helpful. They just become the general gossip, the traffic of your thoughts. If you live in a city, you hear the traffic coming through your windows: there goes a motorcycle, there goes a truck. There goes a car, and then there's somebody shouting. At the beginning you might get involved in or distracted by the noise, but then you begin to think, so what?

Similarly, the traffic of your thoughts and the verbosity of your mind are merely part of the basic chatter that goes on in the universe. Let it go through. You relate to sound, smell, sight, and every experience that you have in the sensorial world with exactly the same mindful approach. You see things simply and directly. You're just there, with them and with your breathing.

Labeling Thinking

It doesn't matter what comes up. You don't have to analyze anything when you are meditating. You can simply maintain your dignified posture and pay attention to your breath. The technique is that you look at the thoughts as they arise and say to yourself, "thinking." Whatever goes through your mind is purely thinking, not mystical experience. Label it thinking and come back to your breath.

So you are there. You are thinking. You don't try to get away from your thoughts, but you don't stick with them or encourage them either. Thought patterns are just ripples on the surface of the pond. They come and they go. They merge into each other, and you take the attitude that they are not a big deal.

Aches and Pains

Bodily aches and pains and physical irritations also come and go. They may seem more problematic than your thoughts. But in meditation practice you regard physical sensations as also thought patterns. Label them thinking. Aches, pains, pins and needles—all thinking. This keeps everything simple and straightforward, so that you can appreciate everything as part of one natural process. There might be a loud noise outside, the sound of a train, traffic, or a jet engine. For that matter, you might be sweating or you might feel cold and chilled. It's all thinking, from this point of view.

When you begin to simplify everything in this way, it allows you to relax. However, often you come up with further complaints. You probably know the story of the princess and the pea. She couldn't sleep because there was a pea under her mattress. You may have a similar experience when you are meditating. You might think there is a little metal ball stuck in your cushion or on your chair that is causing you a lot of pain. Or you feel as if someone is sticking a knife between your shoulder blades. All kinds of discomforts arise. It doesn't matter. The discomfort comes and goes. Just be precise, label it thinking, and return to the breath.

If you take this too far, you could strain your leg, your back, or some other part of your body. So don't ignore the discomfort entirely. Rearrange your posture if it is necessary; it's good to do that at some point. But at the same time it's a thinking process, so relate to it as a thinking process.

Irritation and Exertion

Even though everything is quite simple and straightforward in the practice of meditation, you are still likely to develop irritation. You are getting the best of the best, but you still think that there is something better, something more. It can be very frustrating. At that point, you need to apply exertion. You have to stick with what you have already. You can't ask for more. There's nothing more to give you, in any case! So you have to be content with what you have.

Group Sitting

Many people will receive their initial instruction in a group and may begin their practice of meditation in a group setting. One very helpful thing about practicing meditation with others is that it shows you that you can actually sit for a longer period of time than you imagined. Sitting with a group encourages you to keep going. You find that you can do the meditation, and you can enjoy it, even when it's difficult! When you meditate with a group, the length of the session will be determined for you. Many groups schedule daily or weekly meditation sessions for the same set period of time: twenty minutes, half an hour, forty minutes, or an hour.

I have found that during group retreats of several hours, days, or weeks, it can be helpful to vary the length of the meditation sessions. Not always knowing the length of the sessions can also be good training for you. For example, you might know that you will be practicing meditation from 9 A.M. until noon at your group retreat, but you don't necessarily know how long each meditation session will be. Sometimes you will sit for only fifteen minutes. Other times you might meditate for an hour. This unpredictability encourages you to sit with fewer expectations, and it will help you find out just what your expectations are.

Sitting by Yourself

Daily Practice

If you meditate by yourself, especially when you are trying to establish or maintain a daily meditation practice, it's helpful to have a set time to meditate, usually at the beginning or the end of your day. It's also helpful to have a separate space for meditation in your home or workplace, if you can. The length of your meditation session may vary from day to day, and the length of time may have a lot to do with family and work obligations. If you can only set aside ten or fifteen minutes a day to sit, start with that. You may find that you can set aside more time on the weekends or when you have time off of work. Although the amount of time you sit from day to day may vary, before you start your session each day, it's important to decide how long you're going to sit, and keep to that. If you don't give yourself a set goal, you might give up after five minutes. So decide before you start how long you're going to sit. If you have a meditation instructor, you can also discuss your daily sitting practice with him or her, and come up with a plan to increase the amount you practice each week. Or if you don't have an instructor, you can make your own plan to start with fifteen minutes a day and work up to an hour.

Personal Retreats

You can also do an "in-house" retreat by yourself, where you set aside part of a day or a longer period of time that you can devote to sitting practice. Before you start your retreat, you can write out a schedule for your meditation sessions. If you do an in-house retreat for several days, you can also include meal breaks, readings, and free time in your predetermined schedule. It's good to push yourself a little, in terms of how long you sit, but don't be too ambitious. Be kind to yourself! This is usually something you would only do after you have been practicing meditation for some time.

There is more information on group meditation practice throughout this book. See especially chapter 16, "Touch and Go." For a discussion of personal and group retreats in relationship to aloneness, see chapter 7, "Rhinoceros and Parrot."

Altogether, meditation teaches us that we can handle ourselves—our bodies and our minds—properly. Meditating in this way is thoroughly enjoyable. For the first time we are doing something real, something that is totally free from deception.

4

The Teddy Bear of Breath

The practice of meditation is a process of taming and training. This does not mean immediately calming ourselves or curing our problems. This process is more like training a wild horse or plowing very rocky, hard soil. We should expect lots of challenges, and we have to be willing to go through the whole process.

In order to tame ourselves, body and mind have to be synchronized. First, when you meditate cross-legged on the ground or upright in your chair with a straight back, the body becomes much more workable. Then, once the body has assumed this posture, we have to convince the mind to go along with it. Mind is basically restless and uncertain. So there is a tendency for our minds to shift around a great deal, jumping from one thought to the next.

When this happens, the best way to tame the mind is to give it a toy. The best toy we can provide is something that is similar to the mind. It's not mind itself, but it feels familiar to the mind, almost like a portrait of it. It is like giving a child a doll or a teddy bear, which is small and cuddly and somewhat like the child. It's not too big nor too small, and you can take it to bed with you, or you can throw it around and play with it. You can dress it up and have a tea party with it. It's like an image of yourself, almost like a surrogate.

In meditation, the teddy bear is your breath. Just like the mind, your breathing is by no means still. Of necessity it is somewhat restless. Once you breathe out, you have to breathe in. Once you breathe in, you have to breathe out. That restlessness is similar to how our mind operates, constantly looking for alternatives, constantly generating content. Breathing has a very similar energy to the way the mind operates.

So this toy of breathing is given to the mind. I was taught that only about 25 percent of your concentration should be put on the breath when you're meditating. This is just a rough estimate, so please don't fixate on the percentage. The point is that in this approach, working with breath is just touching the highlights of the breathing. You don't remain completely one with it all the time.

This is very much like a child playing with her teddy bear. When the child is restless or unhappy, she is cheered up by her teddy bear. Then she once again becomes interested in other things. However, there is always something to come back to—her teddy bear. That is your breath.

Putting more attention on the outbreath, which I recommend, is like going down a slide. You slide down, and then you have to walk around and climb the stairs back up the slide, and then you can slide down again. Going down the slide is similar to riding the breath out. When you finish your ride, there's a gap, and you breathe in, which is like climbing back up the slide. Then you ride the breath out again, and there's another gap. This process occurs over and over.

Breathing occupies the mind quite easily. Out and in and in and out happen constantly. Breathing also encourages you to step beyond the emphasis on the body. Your outbreath takes you out into the world. Then naturally you breathe in. Then you want to step out again into the world, so you breathe out. There is a constant process of going in and out. In my tradition this is known as mixing mind and breath together.

The practice of mindfulness meditation is also a way to sharpen your mind. In many cases we are so stunned by the speed and the demands of reality that our minds have become dull. We have lost a lot of our mind's precision, and our perception is somewhat foggy and unclear. Our mental faculties have been overused, overtaxed. Jumping back and forth with thoughts of all kinds and trying to integrate a million thoughts at once makes us numb.

The practice of meditation helps to sharpen our minds and allows us to see and experience things much more directly, by going along with the breathing and getting extraordinarily bored. There is nothing else happening when you practice, other than your breath and your body and the flickering of thoughts and visual entertainment. Even those flickers eventually become somewhat uninteresting.

When the mind has no outside entertainment, interestingly enough, it becomes much sharper. If a child only has one toy, just one teddy bear, then he will know it from top to bottom, from outside to inside. He will completely investigate and memorize the look and feel of every inch of that toy. If you entertain him with hundreds of toys, he'll lose interest in all of them. He'll become cranky and demanding and throw tantrums. So having one thing at a time is better.

When a person begins to work with the outbreath, without any other entertainments, the connection between mind and body becomes very real. Your mind becomes precise and sharp.

The outbreath is like a whetstone, and the mind is like the knife or sword that is being sharpened on that stone. When you sharpen a knife, you draw the blade of the knife across the sharpening stone. Following your outbreath is like drawing the blade of mind across the breath. Then you breathe in, which is like bringing the knife blade back so that you can draw it across the stone again. You always sharpen the blade in the same direction, which is like placing the emphasis on the outbreath over and over again.

When you sharpen a knife, you need a light touch. If you put too much pressure or incorrect pressure on the knife when you draw it across the stone, you may actually dull the blade. Similarly, in working with the breath, trying too hard to stick with mindfulness of breathing can result in feeling hypnotized by the breath or alternatively feeling unable to follow the breath at all. This is one reason that the recommendation is to place only 25 percent of your attention on the breath. You need that kind of light touch to sharpen the mind.

Working with mind, body, and breath in this way is training ourselves in mindfulness. We sometimes think that being mindful means being critical of ourselves and very watchful. We think that meditation provides us with a big brother who is going to watch over us or whip us into shape if we do something wrong. But mindfulness practice is not about punishing yourself when you lose track of your breath or your thoughts. Mindfulness does not criticize or set conditions for you. Nor is it about rewarding you. Rather, it is helping you to discover the alertness that already exists in your mind, by dispelling the dullness that has covered it up.

Working with the breath in your practice of meditation is very important training. It might seem insignificant at first. We might say, "Who doesn't know how to breathe? What's the big deal?" However, sharpening our minds through working with our breathing develops tremendous precision. We often say that meditation practice is about the development of peace. By peace, we mean this experience of being precisely on the dot, which cools down the jumpiness of our minds and the heat of our emotional neurosis. Experiencing this precision is analogous to sitting under a waterfall and letting a cool mountain stream pour onto us, washing away our dirt and sweat. We need to take this shower and relate with the water pouring onto our body from head to toe. That is how we develop peace in meditation.

5

Cool Boredom

In everyday life, we habitually try to conceal the gaps in our experience of mind and body. These gaps are a bit like an awkward silence around the table at a dinner party. A good host is supposed to keep the conversation going with his or her guests, to put them at ease. You might talk about the weather or the latest books you've read or what you are serving for dinner. We treat ourselves similarly. We occupy ourselves with subconscious chatter because we are uncomfortable with any gaps in our conversation with ourselves.

The purpose of the practice of meditation is to experience the gaps. We do nothing, essentially, and see what that brings—either discomfort or relief, whatever the case may be. The starting point for the practice of meditation is the mindfulness discipline of developing peace. The peace we experience in meditation is simply this state of doing nothing, which is experiencing the absence of speed.

Often, in considering the practice of meditation, the question arises as to what you are meditating *on*. In this approach, meditation has no object. You do work with your body, your thoughts, and your breath, but that is different from concentrating wholeheartedly on one thing. Here, you are not meditating upon anything; you are simply being present in a simple way.

The practice works with what is immediately available to you. You have your experience of being alive; you have a mind and you have a body. So you work with those things. You also work with whatever is going through your mind, whatever the content is, whatever the current issues are, whether painful or pleasurable. Whatever you are experiencing, that's where you begin. You also use your breath, which is part of the body and is also affected by mind. Breathing expresses the fact that you are alive. If you're alive, you breathe. The technique is basic and direct: you pay heed to breath. You don't try to use the mindfulness of the breathing to entertain yourself, but you use the mindfulness of breathing to simplify matters.

You develop mindfulness of the rising and falling of the breath. You go along with the process of breathing. In particular, you go along with each exhalation. As the breath goes out, you go out with it. And when the outbreath dissolves, you feel that you are also dissolving. The inbreath is a gap, a space, and then you breathe out again. So there is a constant sense of going out and slowing down.

At the beginning, the technique may be somewhat fascinating, but it quickly becomes boring. You get tired of sitting and breathing, doing nothing again and again and again—and again. You may feel like an awkward fool. It is so uninteresting. You might resent having gotten yourself into this situation. You might also resent the people who encouraged you to do this. You may feel completely foolish, as if the cosmos were mocking you.

Then, as you relax a little bit, you start to call up past experiences, memories of your life as well as your emotions, your aggression and passion. Now you have a private cinema show, and you can review your autobiography while you sit. Then, after a while, you might come back to your breath, thinking that you should try to be a good child and apply the technique.

In meditation we have the opportunity to meet ourselves, to see ourselves clearly for the first time. We have never met ourselves properly or spent this kind of time with ourselves before. Of course, we take time for ourselves; we go off to the country or the ocean for a vacation. But we always find things to do on vacation. We make little handicrafts or we read something. We cook, we talk, we take a walk, or we swim. We never just sit with ourselves. It's a difficult thing to do.

The practice of meditation is not merely hanging out with ourselves, however. We are accomplishing something by being there properly, within the framework of the technique. The technique is simple enough that it doesn't entertain us. In fact, the technique may begin to fall away at some point. As we become more comfortable with ourselves and develop more understanding of ourselves, our application of the technique becomes less heavy-handed. The technique almost seems unnecessary. In the beginning we need the technique, like using a crutch to help us walk when we're injured. Then, once we can walk without it, we don't need the crutch. In meditation it is similar. In the beginning we are very focused on the technique, but eventually we may find that we are just there, simply there.

At that point, we may think that the efficient system we've organized around our practice is breaking down. It can be disconcerting, but it's also refreshing. We sense that there is more to us than our habitual patterns. We have more in us than our bundles of thoughts, emotions, and upheavals. There's something behind this whole façade. We discover the reservoir of softness within ourselves.

At that point, we begin to truly befriend ourselves, which allows us to see ourselves much more honestly. We can see both aspects, not just the bright side of the picture, how fantastic and good we are, but also how terrible we are. Good and bad somehow don't make much difference at this point. It all has one flavor. We see it all.

As your sympathy toward yourself expands, you begin to appreciate and enjoy simply being with yourself, being alone. Or at least you are not as irritated with yourself as you used to be! As you become ever more familiar with yourself, you find that you can actually put up with yourself without complaint—which you have never done before. Your thought patterns, subconscious gossip, and all of your mind's chatter become much less interesting. In fact, you begin to find them all very boring. However, this is slightly different than our normal experience of boredom, because behind the boredom, or even within it, you feel something refreshing: cool boredom. You're bored to death, bored to tears, but it is no longer claustrophobic. The boredom is cooling, refreshing, like the water from a cold mountain stream.

Hot boredom is like being locked in a padded cell. You are bored, miserable, and irritated. You will probably experience lots of that in your meditation practice. Beyond that, however, with cool boredom, you don't feel imprisoned. Cool boredom is quite spacious, and it creates further softness and sympathy toward ourselves. In that space, we are no longer afraid of allowing ourselves to experience a gap. In other words, we realize that existence does not depend on constantly cranking up our egomaniacal machine. There is another way of existing.

6

Gentleness

The practice of meditation allows us to experience the depth of our heart. We discover that our basic being contains gentleness, kindness, and softness. There is a need for such gentleness throughout life. It allows us to be kind to ourselves and to relate openly with others.

Especially if you meditate intensively over a long period of time, you might feel very sad at times, for no particular reason. The process of breathing out, dissolving, and being mindful while you maintain a good seat brings a feeling of sadness and aloneness. You might end up shedding a tear on your meditation cushion. You feel vulnerable and raw. The more you sit, the more you experience this kind of sadness.

Externally you maintain your posture, but inside you begin to dissolve and become like gelatin. You feel jellified and droopy all over. That is a good sign—fantastic, actually. When we practice meditation, we should feel who and what we are. For the first time, you are experiencing yourself as a thoroughly human being. This is how human beings should feel.

We are nothing but human beings, pure human beings, who possess tenderness in our hearts. At the same time, we feel totally bored: tender and bored. You are a real person, a soft person, but also a bored person who doesn't need neurotic problems to entertain or justify him- or herself.

You feel as if you might dissolve into your chair or your meditation cushion. You might become the best jellyfish, the very best. That softness and droopiness might be regarded as corny or unnecessary, but it's good that we feel that way. That softness is in us already. We have that kind of droopiness and those jellyfish-like possibilities of being gentle and soft, raw, without skin, without even bone or marrow.

In meditation we continually rediscover ourselves as authentic human beings who are capable of loving ourselves, and others as well. We are finally beginning to subjugate our intense aggression and toughness. The pretense of toughness is finally being resolved, dissolved, jellified. We find that we can also extend this softness and gentleness to the rest of the world. We can extend ourselves to our father, mother, sisters, brothers, our friends, and to the whole world, the world that we usually hate, the world that irritates us so much. When we look at people, we realize that there is no need to be hateful toward anyone. Our tough exterior is dissolved into a compassionate jellyfish, so soothing, so soft.

This realization only comes from the sitting practice of meditation. Holding our posture, following the breath, working with our thoughts: that is the only way. We begin to find our soft spot, our gentleness. This is one of the best types of gentleness the world has ever experienced. That gentleness is called compassion.

When you look around you, you may see signs in harsh neon lights that say, "Come to our restaurant. We serve the best food." Or "Shop here. You'll get a great bargain." You turn on the television, and there are the ads saying, "Get your money's worth. Only ten dollars." Statements of this nature pop up all over the place in your life. They try to convince you to buy the latest gadget or indulge in the latest fad, whatever it is. You may be interested, even tempted, but regardless of whether you get sucked in to the latest thing or not, you continue to be soft and gentle in relating to your world. You can work directly with such situations in quite a sane way. You don't have to buy someone's aggressive salesmanship. You don't have to bargain them down. You can work with whatever the world offers, without aggression.

The practice of meditation should not lead to an aggressive approach to life. It also shouldn't be an endurance contest or a way to prove yourself. It's not the spiritual version of Outward Bound or of doing pushups. Our approach to meditation has to be ordinary, mundane, and down to earth—directly connected to what we do throughout our lives.

To begin with, every aspect of the practice reflects the continual manifestation of gentleness. You begin to realize that the sound of the meditation bell or timer, to signal the beginning or the end of meditation practice, is the sound of gentleness. Your meditation cushion or the chair that you sit in to meditate is the embodiment of gentleness.

From there, the experience of gentleness begins to affect the rest of your life. Whatever you do in life, you can always find a soft edge, rather than sticking with the hard edges. You find that the entire world is being transformed. In fact, the world stays the same, but you are transformed. And that transforms your experience of the world. It can be done.

From that experience we discover clear vision, perspective, and sharpness, which show us a fresh way to handle the world and relate with our experience as a whole. People think that clarity and brilliance come from having lots of reference points to connect and refer back to. But the truth is that clarity does not need any originator or author at all. Constantly going back and forth between central headquarters and the reference points out in the world makes for a very busy, speedy, and heady journey. It actually makes you dizzy, and then you lose track, in the negative sense. When you drop this drama, it's an extraordinary relief. You don't have to maintain a reference point to your headquarters. You don't have to check back to where you think your mind is coming from. You are left completely loose, open, and fresh. Then there is tremendous clarity, like the sky without clouds. The sun can shine much brighter that way.

This is a personal experience, one that you have to feel before you can fully understand it. However, it is true. It can be done. There can be clarity and brilliance without any reference point, which makes our experience precise, direct, and superior. You are no longer caught up in little problems. You have complete command of the whole situation at that point. It is like rain coming from a cloudless sky. You could actually make rain without having any clouds.

When you have softness and precision at the same time, the lotus of awakened heart is blossoming within you. The lotus always blooms in the mud. You are willing to give birth to this beautiful lotus flower in the muddy waters of your life. For the first time, you realize that you are a candidate to be a wakeful person.

7

Rhinoceros and Parrot

Some of us prefer solitude and individual meditation practice; some of us are drawn to groups. A meditator sitting and practicing meditation alone is like a rhinoceros, which is generally a solitary animal, while a group of meditators practicing together is more like a flock of parrots. These are the two prominent styles of working on oneself in the practice of meditation. Both are valuable, and I would recommend that you combine both approaches, perhaps emphasizing one or the other at various times.

In a sense, rhinoceros and parrot are attitudes that you take, regardless of whether you are practicing alone or with others. When you practice meditation with a group of people, you are still alone. Everybody in the meditation hall is in his or her own little vehicle, which is called a body. There's no room for anybody else in that particular body. Everybody has her own car, her own body—you cannot hitchhike. On the other hand, when you practice by yourself, you are still connected with the community of people who meditate.

You may spend time meditating alone in your home, or you may even do a solitary meditation retreat. A formal solitary retreat can be very valuable, but you need to talk with someone experienced in this kind of retreat practice before you undertake your first retreat. People usually have a meditation teacher who supervises their retreats. It can be a very intense experience, even if you are used to spending time alone.

When you practice alone, it may generate creative energy, and it also generates loneliness. In a solitary retreat, nobody organizes or programs your life, except you. So there is both freedom and demand. You have to improvise everything for yourself. Being in solitude is like a love affair: Sometimes you like it; sometimes you don't like it at all. The echo of aloneness is always there. You have no opportunity, none whatsoever, to indulge in anything. There are no candy stores or movie theaters. You are just being by yourself, just simply being you, at that point.

To develop a real feeling for community, at least in terms of a community of meditators, you need to have experienced loneliness and aloneness. We reject that idea. We don't want to be alone. Being with others makes us feel secure. We want to have someone to call. We always want to have a phone, so that our friends can reach us and we can reach them if we feel isolated.

The point of being alone is not so much to experience nature by appreciating the beauties of the sunrise and the sunset, the chirping of birds, or the diversity of leaves, trees, rocks, and brooks in the countryside. Those things are delightful, of course, but being in retreat or in solitude is just about being alone, completely alone. You can do a solitary retreat in an apartment in the middle of Los Angeles.

You came into this world alone. Newborn babies are quite helpless. It's quite lonely for them. You feed them and change their diapers, you give them love and nurturing, you care for them, but all of that is an expression of loneliness, as far as the baby is concerned. A child is still alone, even with its parents.

There is an echo of loneliness when a child calls out: "Mommy, Daddy!" There's an aspect of warmth and love, of course, but when that powerful little voice calls out, "Daddy! Mommy!" that little voice is filled with loneliness.

It's the same thing when you die. You are going to leave this world alone. If you die in a hospital, you may be surrounded by doctors, friends, and relatives. They may be afraid to admit to themselves that you're going to die, let alone to tell you, or they may decide to tell you that you're in bad shape and you might die. All of that is an expression of loneliness, that you are alone.

Of course, other people are also alone and have to go through this, but that doesn't particularly help. You are one single individual experiencing this world. Sharing opinions, attitudes, practices, and all sorts of disciplines with others is not regarded as security. A group of people working together is still working with aloneness.

This could actually be very promising, but we usually regard it as a problem. When we feel lonely, we try to recruit other people so that we can forget our loneliness. We fall in love, we recruit sympathizers, we read books, we listen to music, we cook a good meal: those are often expressions of rejecting our loneliness. This failure to acknowledge and accept our aloneness is the source of the most fundamental confusion in the world. It keeps confusion spinning: trying to escape from ourselves and not accepting aloneness.

The point of the practice of meditation is to relate to that big problem. Simple aloneness is nondual. Trying to escape from aloneness produces duality. We produce the illusion of something that is *other* than us, so that the other can entertain us constantly.

You don't practice meditation and you don't do a retreat to prove something to yourself or to others. You don't do it to show how committed or macho you are. Some people are very proud of all the retreat practice they do: "I did a retreat for ten days!" "That's nothing. I did three months." "I did a whole year!" "I did four years!" Whatever . . . So what? Finally, ultimately, we are alone with the echo of our loneliness, so we can't really impress anybody at all. You might report your exertion and your achievement, but no one is really impressed. Your glorious report is still an expression of loneliness. Understanding loneliness as the basic premise of solitary practice is extremely important. You are alone and lonely, and you can't escape from that situation.

Strangely enough, sometimes loneliness is described as union. That might sound hopeful, but in this context union is not about uniting that and this and living happily ever after. In terms of your loneliness, union is about indivisibility. If you are really properly lonely, you might recognize that situations are indivisible. They can't be divided up into this and that or you and other. It's not that everything is one. Everything is zero. That is the realization that comes from experiencing loneliness.

When a lonely person has some acceptance of his or her aloneness, it can actually be very spacious. Then a person can relate directly to other lonely people. Many lonely people are confused because they don't accept aloneness. You can help others to see that loneliness is part of their innate nature, and you can encourage lonely individuals to get together and create a community that practices meditation together.

At that point, having worked with your own aloneness, you need to join the flock of parrots. In this flock, people don't provide one another with false security. Actually, making friends with other practitioners constantly reminds us of our original loneliness. At least we have that in common! When lonely individuals work together and practice together, it produces enormous energy and vigor, because the energy is not conditioned. It is not about establishing security or ground as such.

Accepting our loneliness and working with it could be very romantic, even heroic. We should appreciate and praise the beauty of being in solitude, whether we are alone with ourselves or alone with others. You can't solve your basic problem of loneliness. It is always there. The good news is that it is the seed of wisdom.

8

The Present Moment

One of the effects of meditation is that you become more open-minded, and this gives rise to an interest in working with others. In that way, meditation practice can transform your lifestyle and your relationships with other people. Then, mindfulness practice becomes a reference point in dealing with the rest of the world. So we should look further at how to relate with the experience of everyday life.

Sometimes we talk about the "post-meditation" experience, which refers to our experience after we meditate. We could say that it extends to our experience of our work life and our home life—the boardroom and the kitchen sink—when that experience is influenced by mindfulness.

Beyond that, by applying mindfulness in post-meditation, or mindfulness in action, you begin to transcend or break down the boundary between meditating and not meditating. The benefits of meditation also begin to help you in your daily life. Daily problems and the pain of daily life may often feel almost poisonous. However, meditative awareness can help you to convert that poison into medicine, the medicine of cheerful-ness. You begin to develop the ability to transform difficulties into delight, something delightfully workable. This transforma-tion comes from appreciating your life, including its irritations and challenges.

In order to work with difficulties from a mindful perspec-tive, you need to be present in your life. So it is important not to dwell too much on your memories. You may have good memories or bad ones. Whatever has occurred, whether plea-surable or painful, you can't reside in that memory, or you will be stuck in the past. The basic thrust is to live in the present situation.

The present is direct and straightforward. Your experience of it is heightened through mindfulness. When you are mindful of your breath in meditation, when you are mindful of your thoughts, or when you are mindful of going from the practice of meditation to dealing with the kitchen sink, all those situa-tions are in the present. You don't borrow ideas from the past, and you don't try to fundraise from the future. You just stay on the spot, now.

That may be easy to say, but it's not so easy to do. We often find it satisfying to have a reference point to what might hap-pen in the future or what has happened in the past. We feel more relaxed when we can refer to past experiences to inform what is happening now. We borrow from the past and anticipate the future, and that makes us feel secure and cozy. We may think we are living in the present, but when we are preoccupied with past and future, we are blind to the current situation.

Living in the present may seem like quite a foreign idea. What does that even mean? If you have a regular schedule, a nine-to-five job, you cycle through your weekly activities from Monday to Friday, doing what is expected of you and what you expect of yourself. If something out of the ordinary occurs, something that is completely outside of the routine of your Monday-to-Friday world, it can be quite disconcerting.

We are bewildered when something unexpected pops up. A flea jumps on your nose. What should you do? You swat at it or you ignore it if you can. If that doesn't work, then you search for a memory from the past to help you cope. You try to remember how you dealt with the last flea that landed on you. Or you may try to strategize how you'll prevent insects from bothering you in the future. None of that helps much. We can be much more present if we don't pay so much attention to the past or the expectations of the future. Then, we might discover that we can enjoy the present moment, which is always new and fresh. We might make friends with our fleas.

A lot of us find it difficult to make decisions. It seems sensible, responsible, to base our decisions on what happened in the past or what is likely to occur in the future. On the other hand, we would like to be more spontaneous, but the idea of making a decision based on the present moment seems almost incomprehensible. Looking at the process of decision making may help us to understand how to be in the present moment in everyday life.

I can't tell you exactly how you should make decisions, because it's a very personal thing. I can tell you what I do myself. I wouldn't suggest that you mimic or copy me, particularly, but you might find my approach helpful. When I have to make a decision, I look closely at what is occurring right now, at the very point when I have to make up my mind. The idea is to approach looking at the situation with a complete freshness of mind. After that, consideration and responsibility come into play.

Sometimes people ask my advice. Someone comes to me and asks, "I have this problem. What should I do?" I look at the person's face, at the messenger of the problem and how he or she manifests. I look directly at how the person presents the problem. From that I develop some understanding about what is really going on, on the spot. Only then do I ask the person what the case history of the situation is or what he or she thinks might happen in the future. The past and the future are like the cosmetics, so to speak, on the present situation. Then, when you put all that input together, you make your decision accordingly.

Sometimes, after all that, you still don't have any idea how to proceed. You are still bewildered. You haven't come up with an answer, for yourself or anyone else. If you meet the situation directly, if you engage it and look at it straight on, you will discover some idea of what to do.

Ultimately, decisions don't just come from the present, either. There's another twist, which we call the fourth moment. There is past, present, and future, and then there's the fourth moment, beyond that. It's a gap. Your decisions could actually come from that gap. I suppose this sounds rather esoteric.

When you reach a critical juncture, you ask yourself, "Should I turn right or left? Here I am at the fork in the road." What should you do? If you pay enough attention to that fork in the road, there will be a gap, and you will develop some feeling for how things *are,* and whether you should go left or right. Then, you will develop some feeling for the present situation, and you can also look at the past and the future, to make sure that your decision is a good one. But first, there has to be a direct connection with what is happening now. Otherwise, if you purely study the case history of the situation, that will lead to failure and bankruptcy in almost every case.

Being in the present, as opposed to living in the past or the future, is an important way that mindfulness helps to clarify the problems that we experience in our everyday lives. Bringing everything into the present allows us to purify or transform our habitual patterns and preconceptions.

Almost every great religious or spiritual tradition has techniques for purifying yourself to overcome problems or difficulties. Some traditions make use of contemplation, meditation, or prayer as forms of purification. Some approaches are based on a physical discipline, such as special diets or yoga. Physical purification is like being put in a washing machine, but then you discover that the washing machine is you. Or the approach to purity may be more like sitting in a sauna. The longer you sit in that atmosphere, the more the pores in your skin are going to open, so that you can clean out all the dirt.

Some forms of purification are severe, like exposing a wound to the air, or even washing it with water or vinegar to remove the germs. Some methods or rituals of physical purification may involve intentionally inflicting pain on yourself, such as walking on hot coals. When you have suffered enough pain, the absence of pain brings tremendous relief. When there is a gap in the pain, you feel so relieved and relaxed. You experience a gap in your self-centeredness. That approach underlies many mystical traditions. The practice of mindfulness may lead to a similar experience of a moment free from habitual thought, but it begins with an understanding that the purity is already there, within you. From that point of view, there is nothing to purify; therefore, you don't have to deliberately inflict pain on yourself.

Of course, sometimes you may find the practice of meditation painful. If you're used to sitting in a chair and you decide to meditate on a cushion, the cross-legged posture may be uncomfortable. You may experience back pains when you meditate, or all kinds of physical discomfort, as well as visual or auditory distractions and extreme states of mind. None of that is regarded as a problem, something that you have to solve. We are not starting with the view that we are bad and we're trying to compensate for that by being good. In the practice of mindfulness, we are simply trying to let our basic quality of goodness shine through. So although you might find the practice painful at times, the pain that you experience is more like labor pain. It is as though you're about to give birth to a child.

Mindfulness is working toward uncovering self-existing kindness and goodness. It may take a lot of breakthroughs; it may be painful to uncloud the sky in order to see the sun properly. But you can do it.

As we discussed in earlier chapters, your journey begins with personal appreciation, with kindness, gentleness, and making friends with yourself. The more we trust ourselves, the more we acknowledge our friendship with ourselves, the more we uncover gentleness and kindness throughout our lives. That is the only way to overcome the fundamental obstacles in our lives. The breakthroughs won't come from combat. We won't uncover peacefulness by going to war with ourselves or others. We don't have to attack anybody, kill anybody, or destroy anybody in order to feel better about ourselves. The obstacle of self-hatred will fall away, by itself, when we have trust in ourselves. In that way, the experience of mindfulness can transform pain into freedom.

Finally, we begin to feel that who we are and what we are is worthwhile. We are doing the right thing. We are being completely honest with ourselves, in spite of the temptation to deceive ourselves. Still we are here. We are doing our job fully, properly, and we are so delighted. Because of that delight, we can free ourselves. Freedom comes with a feeling of both dignity and of sadness, which help us to remain genuine.

If we regard our problems as attacks from the outside, if we think that struggle or revolution is the solution, we are perpetuating aggression, and we can't free ourselves, let alone help anyone else. We don't gain freedom by fighting or paying our jailers to liberate us from our confusion. The more we think that liberation is based on aggression, the more we imprison ourselves and those we are trying to help. Rather, the only way to free ourselves is to be kind to ourselves and kind to the rest of the world. With that approach, we can do an excellent job.

So the domestic, psychological, and sociological difficulties and irritations in everyday life are not regarded as imprisonment. There might be all kinds of inconvenience. When you want to meditate, you might be stuck with a screaming baby, and you might not be able to afford a babysitter. On your way to an important meeting, your car breaks down and you need to take a taxi, but you don't have the money for the cab. All kinds of situations like that will arise, but none of them are unworkable. Rather, life requires a sense of humor. There are always going to be problems. In fact, it would be very suspicious if things were smooth all the time.

It's better not to be a millionaire. If you are rich, you may think you can pay your way into heaven. You think you can take a helicopter to the enlightened world. But it doesn't work that way. You have to improvise and do things manually in life. You have the choice and the chance to convert your problems into promises. Hopefully, you will take advantage of this opportunity.

9

The Bridge of Compassion

In the previous chapter we discussed the connection between our sitting practice of meditation and our day-to-day experience. On the one hand, there is your familiar everyday life. You know it quite well. You can see it clearly, filled with all the things that you have to handle in your life. On the other hand, you have your comfortable or uncomfortable meditation. Meditation could give you an inkling of self-indulgence, of feeling self-satisfied. To remedy that, mindfulness also extends to the domestic situations of life, the kitchen-sink problems that we face constantly. Practically speaking, however, how do we link our meditation with the everyday challenges that we face all the time? How do we build a bridge between the sitting practice of meditation and meditation in action, or the post-meditation practice of mindfulness in everyday life?

In order to communicate from one side of the bridge to the other side, a sympathetic attitude is required, an attitude of charity, in the original sense of that word. The word *charity* is derived from Latin and Sanskrit words for warmth and love.

That is the real meaning of compassion: fundamental warmth. That, too, is the link between meditation practice and everyday life.

The practice of meditation is about trusting yourself. As the practice becomes a more prominent feature of your daily life, you not only learn to trust yourself but you might begin to actually love yourself, or to have a compassionate attitude toward yourself. As much basic space as you discover in your practice, there is that much *warmth* in the space as well. There's a delightful feeling of positive things happening in you, constantly. Your meditation is no longer mechanical or a drag, but it is a delightful thing to do. Meditation is making friends with yourself.

Having made friends with yourself in the practice of meditation, you can't just contain that warmth within yourself. You have to have an outlet for it. That outlet is communication with the world outside, with the other side of the bridge. Compassion acts as the bridge. Otherwise, it *is* possible that your practice of meditation might become self-satisfying. It might even become aggressive: "Don't touch me. I know what I'm doing. Just let me meditate!" You might become like an arrogant professor who thinks that she knows everything. If you ask her a question that she thinks is stupid, she will get angry at you rather than trying to answer your question. So if you exclusively practice meditation with no element of compassion in it, that kind of self-contained, self-satisfying practice could contain aggression.

Compassion is not logical. It's basically spacious and generous. A compassionate person might not be sure whether he is being compassionate to you or whether you are being compassionate to him, because compassion creates a total environment of generosity. Generosity is implied; it just happens, rather than *you* making it happen. It's just there, without direction, without me, without "for them." It's full of joy, a spontaneously existing grin of joy, constant joy.

This joy also contains wealth and richness. Compassion could be said to be the ultimate attitude of richness. It is anti-poverty, the ultimate war on want. It contains all sorts of heroic, juicy, positive, visionary, expansive, bigger-scale thinking. It is a much bigger way of relating to yourself and to your world, your projections.

The attitude of compassion is a larger way of thinking, thinking on a larger scale. The attitude is one of being born rich rather than becoming rich. It is a world of plenty.

Without compassion, meditation cannot be transferred into action at all. We have a tendency, which almost feels automatic, to freeze up, to keep things frozen within ourselves. We preserve things in ourselves because we are afraid of losing them, afraid of losing our wealth. When we begin to experience fundamental warmth in our practice of meditation, that generous attitude and experience invite us to relate more openly with people. We begin to thaw out. People are no longer regarded as a drain on our energy at all. People recharge our energy. They make us feel wealthy, rich, plentiful.

When you have to perform difficult tasks in your life, which may involve dealing with difficult people, you no longer feel that you are running out of resources. Each time a difficult task is presented to you, it's a delightful chance to demonstrate your richness, your wealth. With that attitude, you no longer draw into yourself or pull away. Rather, you become generous and available. Meditation in action, which we can also call mindfulness in action, comes from this mentality of richness. From this point of view, there is no poverty.

Something is lacking in meditation if there is no compassion in it. Then meditation becomes isolated and unrelated. You feel orphaned with no father or mother to take care of you. You feel abandoned, and you cut yourself off from the world, because you don't like the rest of the world.

So we need the bridge of compassion, to connect our meditation practice with everyday life. The cultivation of compassion begins with experiencing a cooling off of passion and aggression in the sitting practice of meditation. Passion implies urgency: you want to acquire something right now to satisfy your desire. When there's less desire, there's also less aggression and speed. The moment you start to relate to simplicity in the practice of meditation, you don't have to rush anymore. You're self-contained in that sense. Because you're not in a hurry, you can afford to relax. Then you can get to know yourself, and eventually you begin to love yourself. That is the source of warmth and compassion. It's quite simple, from that point of view.

Everything that arises in your meditation practice, all the thoughts and emotions, lend an earthy quality to meditation practice. Meditation practice is realistic—it takes place in the real world, rather than on some ethereal plane. This earthiness in your practice is also embryonic compassion, because compassionate warmth is grounded. It's not in a hurry. It is not being hasty but instead relating to each situation in life as it is. There was a famous Native American leader in the nineteenth century, Sitting Bull, whose name is a vivid example of the earthiness of compassion. That name implies something solid, organic, and definite. It exemplifies definitely being there, resting.

Action without compassion is like planting a dead tree. It will never grow. But any action that contains compassion is planting a living tree that grows endlessly and never dies. Or even if the tree dies, it always leaves a seed behind, which will grow into another tree. That organic quality of compassion goes on and on and on.

You don't have to nurse compassion. It is like making yogurt. You add the culture to milk, and then you keep the milk warm until it becomes yogurt. Sometimes you try to speed the yogurt along by increasing the temperature of the milk. But that usually doesn't make good yogurt at all. If you had left it at the right temperature and just abandoned it for a while, it would have made good yogurt.

Similarly, you needn't constantly micromanage your life. Disowning is necessary at a certain point. You don't have to constantly meddle in situations that don't require further maintenance. Part of compassion is trust. If something positive is happening, you don't have to check up on it all the time. The more you check up, the more possibilities there are of interrupting the growth. It requires fearlessness to let things be. In a sense, it's a form of positive thinking. It's the true mentality of wealth and richness.

Fear comes from panic and the bewilderment of uncertainty, which is related to lack of trust in oneself. You feel inadequate to deal with the mysterious situations that constantly seem to be threatening you. If you have a compassionate relationship with yourself, you trust yourself and you know what you are doing, at least fundamentally. Your projections, which are just a mirror reflection of yourself, become methodical or predictable, so you know how to relate to a situation and also how to leave it alone. Then there is no more fear.

There's a distinction between emotional compassion and direct compassion. Ultimately, you don't have to *feel* compassion. You just *be* compassion. If you are open to situations, compassion just happens, because you are not wrapped up in self-indulgency at that point. You don't have to maintain compassion, but you acknowledge it. That is the mentality of richness: acknowledging that the bridge of compassion is there and available. You don't have to do more than that.

Meditation without concepts, without sidetracks of any kind, is our practice. Within that basic practice there should be a friendly attitude toward oneself as well as a sense of radiating that friendliness. This friendliness can permeate our environment, which includes our living situation and all the people in our lives.

Compassion also contains wisdom, which is a primordial intelligence. We could say that it is discovering unoriginated, or primordial, trust in ourselves. We don't have to logically work out that trust. It is there already. In some sense, it has no beginning. It is a kind of wisdom eye that we innately possess.

Part Two

Foundations of
Mindfulness

10

First Thought

In Part One, we explored the meaning of making friends with ourselves in the practice of meditation and in life in general. The basic practice of mindfulness meditation was introduced, and we looked at some of the most important components of that practice, such as working with the breath, as well as the experiences of gentleness, cool boredom, aloneness, and the discovery of compassion. Now in Part Two, we will delve more deeply into this thing called "mind"—as in the word *mindful*—and investigate the qualities that characterize mindfulness and lead to its maturation. These aspects of mindfulness also provide us with the foundation, or the ground, for our practice. Additionally, they show us ways that our practice may deepen and evolve.

It is often said that meditation is concerned with taming and training the mind, but what do we mean by that word *mind*? Many philosophical, psychological, and spiritual preconceptions arise when we try to define mind or consciousness, and they can get in the way when we're working directly with the practice of meditation. If we want to find out more directly what meditation is and what happens when we meditate, we might want to ask, "*Who* is meditating?" This will get us into the nitty-gritty of what we mean by mind. To understand what we are doing when we meditate, the seed or the fundamental question is "Who are we?"

Ask yourself that question, "Who am I?" You may find that you don't have an answer. From that non-answer, that simple gap or open space, you may experience a flash of who you are. I refer to that glimpse as "first thought." That first thought may be a realization of confusion or neurosis, not necessarily a pleasant or highly evolved thought. It is an unconditioned reaction or thought. There's a gap, and then there's this first thought.

That first thought is not regarded as a particularly enlightened thought, but it *is* a true thought. It is your raw-and-ruggedness. It might reflect confusion or insight. This first thought may be shocking, or it may be quite complimentary. Don't ask too many questions about it. Just let it be there as your first thought.

We're usually circumspect about the first thought we come across, so we drum up a second, more reasoned, thought. This second thought reviews the first and makes us feel safer, more legitimate. Sometimes we don't even trust *that* thought. So we go out of our way to ask someone—a parent, teacher, or perhaps a friend—to reassure us that our insight is legitimate: "I have this thought, but I don't know whether it's good or not. What do you think?"

We have created layer after layer of these security mechanisms. In fact, life often encourages us to do things this way. We are taught to consult authorities or experts about almost everything. If you feel sick, you ask a professional for advice, who is called a doctor. If you feel mentally unwell, you ask a professional called a psychiatrist or a therapist to help you. If you have a leak in the roof or something is wrong with the plumbing in your house, you call in a professional roofer, a plumber, or a general contractor to fix the problem. In our practice of meditation, this need for professional advice may lead us to reject our first thought.

First thought is an intuition that we pick up on in ourselves, but we often don't accept it. We're not prepared to accept our own experience without outside validation. We ask ourselves, "What is the proof?" Or we ask, "Is it okay to feel this way? If I go along with this first thought, something might go terribly wrong. Then what?" That second-guessing of ourselves is precisely the problem, the second thought that gets in the way.

First thought is a direct experience before good, bad, and indifferent arise. You are still in "no-man's-land." The area is not yet occupied by *this* or *that*. There is still a field of openness.

Working with first thought is not a matter of practicing something or rehearsing something until you get good at it. It is much more immediate than that. It is a spontaneous starting point. First thought is a flash or a spark of what you are about, who you are, and what you are. On the spot, you can rediscover your mind, what your mind might be, what your mind really is.

The approach of seeing "first thought as best thought," a phrase that I coined for accepting the workability of our first thought, is a very ordinary, sensible way of looking at oneself and finding out what one's mind is. Do we have a mind at all or not? Look and see. That first thought, the first thing you see, is your mind. The experience of first thought happens simply and directly. It is not some higher ideal state. Rather, in order to begin training the mind, we need to start with seeing the basic ground, the foundation.

The only way to find out who we are is to just look. There you are. You might hate what you see or you might love it. So what? That's it. That's you. That's good old you. That is the basic mind that we're talking about. Look at you and find out about you. Just look.

What you find doesn't particularly lead to ecstasy or depression. You know yourself already anyway. The basic point is to have an attitude of openness toward who you are, what you are. You might want to ask me or someone else whether what you discover is good or bad. My response is "No comment." We haven't gotten to the level of good and bad. We have to find out who we are at the beginning. We really have to look into that.

In your everyday life or as part of your upbringing, you may have been told that you should try to be good before you had any idea who you are. This just creates obstacles for you. If you try to reform yourself before you look into who you are, you already feel condemned; you feel terrible. That approach undermines your intelligence, sharpness, and insightfulness. You can be crippled by condemnation. "You don't know how to carry yourself. Try to be more graceful." Or, "Try to be intelligent." If you follow that advice, you end up with no idea who you actually are or who is doing those recommended things. So before we acquire any of those affectations, so to speak, we need to examine ourselves. Or, if we've already been conditioned in that way, we need to let go of that baggage. The way to do that, or at least to begin to do that, is simply to see our first thought. And that's why it's the best thought, because it comes before any discussion of good and bad.

The word *best* here is neutral; it's about fundamental insight and energy. It is the best flash you can have of who you are, without any reference point. It doesn't tell you whether you are a good person or a bad person.

On a very ordinary level, if someone asks you who you are, you might give her your name and tell her where you were born. You provide that kind of information when you fill out a form to apply for a passport or a visa to visit another country. However, that kind of information is irrelevant here. We're planning to settle down in our own country, in our own spot, and practice meditation where we are.

When we look inside ourselves and examine what we feel, we might discover that there is something in ourselves that feels "I am myself." You feel yourself so powerfully, so strongly. It seems that there is no other choice: "I feel that I am what I am, beyond even my name. I feel my thing-ness inside me. I feel me!"

This is fundamentally an emotional statement. If you feel lonely, you make a statement of your aloneness: "I am what I am, all by myself." If you are angry, you assert yourself in another way as "me." "I'm angry and I have the right to fight, to show my stuff and share my story line with the object of my anger." If you feel lustful or passionate, you want your lover to acknowledge you. "I feel so passionate. You should surrender to me. We have to work things out together." In all of these cases, the main point is "I am what I am. I have this strong message of me, which I'm going to tell you."

You have this first strong flash of who you are, acknowledging yourself before you do anything further. Then you might try to be generous to another person. You might say, "Maybe you would like to say something about me? Please come and say it!" You become more ingratiating, but that's largely an afterthought. We try to show interest in what others think about us or even think about themselves. That interchange, however, just whets your appetite to talk more about yourself with your friends. You want to get together with someone again because the discussion makes you feel very powerful. To continue the dialogue, you might try to make a deal: "You can make me happy, and I will make you happy!" Or, "You can make me feel wretched, and I'll make you feel wretched." Or, "Let's have a duel, a fight to the death."

What is that really about? It is about discovering *this*, this particular point, *this*, this thing that is highly strung like a wild horse or a paranoid dog. *This* is in us; this is us. It is so tough and so seductive. It is sometimes extremely good and sometimes extremely wicked. We have this thing, we talk about this thing, and this thing that we are talking about is *mind*, obviously. We are not talking about our body or our situation in life. We are talking about our mind.

The definition of mind being used here is "that which experiences the sense of separateness." As long as that attitude of this-ness is involved, there is also the otherness, automatically. *That* could not survive without *this,* and vice versa. We are always hanging on to something or other; that something is called mind. Mind in this sense also has a quality of heart, actually, because our emotions and connections to others are involved.

The fundamental idea of mind here is "that which feels the need for something"—the need to reinforce your existence. We are eagerly looking for enemies and lovers in life, to different degrees. That's what it boils down to. Your enemy is not necessarily someone you hate to the nth degree. You don't even have to feel totally sick of that person. On the other side, you don't have to be in love with everyone you like. There are large areas of love and hate, and sometimes it's a mixed bag. The borderlines are mixed up. The main emphasis is your need to reinforce your strength. You can show your enemies or your friends that you are a powerful person. If you strike somebody, literally or metaphorically, that person has to acknowledge you, and you hope that he or she will give in to you. Or a person could be seduced and come into your territory and begin to give in to you that way, in the realm of passion or desire.

This description of mind relates to a psychological description of ego or egotism. The term *ego* can be used to describe ego-mania, which is self-indulgence and a style of self that is looking for security and survival, trying to establish the certainty of one's existence. That is the confused and aggressive part of ego, which is completely blind. However, there is also another view of ego as intelligence and being assertive in a positive sense. When we speak of mind here, we're not only talking about the negative side of ego. Mind is just awareness that exists within our being. It is awareness that is capable of relating with reference points of all kinds. Passion and aggression, love and hate, are included in those reference points, but the basic idea of mind here is that which is capable of experiencing reference points altogether. It is just a mechanical thing.

Mind in this sense is like using your antennae. It is a basic mechanism, although the idea of mind being mechanical dilutes its power somewhat. It is basic intelligence, something constant, which exists in us all the time. *Then* we begin to color it, by saying that if that or this is the case, we want to change ourselves in *this* way or *that* way. After the first thought, you begin to change your mind—which is second thought. You begin to make it into something else, rather than acknowledging what you have actually seen.

When we use the word *mind* as a noun, it sounds static, somewhat isolated from action. The verb form *minding* expresses the sense of mind as a continual activity. Your mind is minding constantly. It is constantly looking for a reference point, looking for a connection to something. Why is that? Fundamentally, in spite of all our assertions of "me-ness," we fear that we may not exist. We feel inadequate. We don't feel so good about ourselves, basically.

Your sense of self is like a hat you see in a store window. You think it looks fantastic and you want to buy it, so you go into the store and ask the salesperson to show it to you. When you can actually hold it, try it on, and look at it up close, it turns out that it's not so great. You feel that you were conned. You change your mind about that fantastic hat.

Similarly, you may say, "I'm having a fantastic life. I'm doing lots of exciting things and having a great time. I feel terrific; I feel like a new person." Sure. Still . . . Why do we have to keep telling ourselves those things again and again? Why? If everything is so amazing already, there is no reason to say so and to reflect back, again and again, on those highlights. Why do you need to reassure yourself? That need for reassurance is precisely the point: We feel that something is leaking, but we don't want to acknowledge it as such. There is a hole somewhere in our life that we try to plug up. All our posturing is a sign that we are just about to realize that we don't exist in the way we thought we did. We actually know that intuitively. Yet we keep on trying to prove ourselves to ourselves, to ensure that we will survive.

In the practice of meditation and contemplative discipline in general, it is important to admit at the beginning that this fortress, or shrine, of our self-existence doesn't hold true. If we are honest with ourselves, we may realize that we are trying to turn a sand castle into a permanent structure. It keeps getting washed away, but we make many attempts to rebuild the castle, hoping to reassure ourselves. Many people use meditation to make themselves feel better or more uplifted. Some people like the idea of a spiritual search because if we are searching for something, at least we have purpose in our lives. But *search* here is a euphemism for uncertainty and panic.

You may tell yourself that you'll find something, once you begin to search. You *can* exist. You don't have to give anything up after all. You will get something out of your search. You slowly sneak in the back door of your existence so that you can retain your hard-line individuality. You say to yourself, "I can stay on top of the world. I can become a little dictator in the name of my achievement of mindfulness."

To avoid that problem, we have to look very closely into what mind is and how our minds function. There are all kinds of holes in us. Even when we acknowledge them, we might still try to create a patchwork to cover them up. You think you've exposed yourself and become a completely pure, clean, and reasonable person. You've penetrated all the deceptions. You've seen all the holes in your logic. But if you then try to sew patches over the holes, it becomes an endless game.

The alternative is first thought: continually looking closely and acknowledging exactly what is happening. When you practice meditation, you need to understand your motivation and look at what you are doing. How are you going to work with yourself? Exposing oneself to oneself without pretense and without patches is the real working ground and the genuine motive for practice.

11

Appreciation

The discipline of meditation is a dignified approach to learning how to be here. Engaging in a practice that is so definite, concrete, and personal brings a feeling of joy. This is somewhat selfless joy, because it is not glorifying anybody, oneself or others. You are just appreciating that you have made a genuine connection to the practice of meditation and to yourself.

Experiencing the fresh first thought, as we discussed in the previous chapter, has enabled you to discover something basic about who you are, what you are. We shouldn't exaggerate that experience. In meditation, you don't try to jazz things up because you are in a bad state of mind or in bad spirits. You don't have to pretend that life is a fantastic rose garden where everything is pleasurable. The practice of meditation is sometimes presented as a way to achieve a blissful state of mind or as a form of positive thinking. However, you don't have to convince yourself that meditation is a good thing to do. You don't have to suppress your conflicted feelings or questions. You don't have to build yourself up. You can simply appreciate.

Genuine appreciation is acknowledging yourself as a person who is committed to the practice of meditation and to the basic mindfulness and awareness that arise from the practice and continue throughout the rest of your life. It is simple appreciation of a sense of being. Physically, you are sitting in a chair or on your meditation cushion. You are practicing mindfulness. You are here. That is enough.

When you are sitting on the floor or in a chair meditating, it is a simple situation. No mystical connotations apply here. You are here, sitting on the earth, quite rightly so. There's a physical awareness that you are meditating, and there is mental awareness, which includes all your mental states, including your daydreaming world. Once you make the commitment to practice, it's a total commitment, which includes the psychological aspect of things. Your thoughts may wander around all over the continent, to Alaska or Mexico, Vancouver or New York City. Nevertheless, in actual fact, you are here. Being psychologically present may be a big project, but it helps that you are physically here in your body.

When you practice meditation, you should sit without a plan. It should be meaningful without it being a big deal. You simply sit on the floor or in your chair. If you question whether you are sitting properly or not, then you might begin to perch. Instead, just sit, very simply and directly. If you are waiting for something to happen, that is a problem of future orientation. If you are oriented to the present, you just do it. It's a very blunt approach to life, blunt and realistic. There's no romance involved, except for the joy of the present.

You feel that you are there, you are breathing, you are sitting. You feel your head, your shoulders, and your arms. You don't have to go through a special sequence or program of building up your awareness. Keep it extremely simple. There is almost a quality of carelessness. It's not frivolity or mindlessness, but a positive experience of relaxation and not overthinking what you're doing. You just sit and do it.

When people decide to do a long group meditation retreat, over a number of days, weeks, or months, they come to such a retreat with many ideas about what they're going to achieve. They bring a lot of questions about what they're doing, why they're doing it, and how they will benefit from the retreat. During the retreat, they throw those questions back on themselves. They could decide to leave the retreat anytime. They are not required by anyone to stay. Strangely, although many people lose heart at some point during the retreat, they usually stay through the whole thing. And they usually regain their heart. They may feel quite heroic when they finish. People meditate for many days with no promise and no particular purpose, but still they do it.

At the beginning, they may have many ambitions, but then something turns that around. Their expectations begin to fall apart, through the practice of meditation. Someone who is seriously interested in meditation should not expect any feedback or promises from the practice. Most people come to realize that the point of the sitting practice of meditation is just to sit, to actually sit properly. The complications of thought patterns and confusion of all kinds about the technique—no matter how these thoughts arise, no matter how meaningful or devastating they may seem, and no matter how they dissolve or go away—are all just mental creations rather than meditative insights as such.

When you practice meditation, you have a choice. You can take the attitude that you are just doing it, or you can take the attitude that you are waiting for something to happen. Maybe you think *nothing* will happen, but you still secretly think that nothing is "it." So you're still waiting for something or other. The other attitude is just to be, which is the recommended approach. One should just sit and be.

A great teacher of meditation once said, "Meditating is trying to look at your own eyes without using a mirror." That's a very mysterious statement. How can we look at our own eyes without a mirror? The idea stops us in our tracks. But maybe we can explore that in our practice. The only way to solve this riddle is just to be there.

"Nowness" is a good word to describe the experience of simply being present. There is no other reference point involved. You might think that nowness is a choice between now and then or between this and that. But the state of nowness is choiceless. *Now* includes emptiness and nonexistence as well as fullness, all at the same time. Now is powerful because it doesn't have any connections with past or future. We might feel threatened by now, because we prefer to stick with what has occurred or what might occur. We have difficulty ungluing ourselves from past and future. It's not particularly pleasant to be now. It is demanding, but it is also very genuine.

In the practice of meditation, the development of peace is the expression of nowness. Peace is the experience of simplicity rather than pleasure or happiness as such. We are not discussing lofty ideas about peace, such as peace on earth. Being in a state of peace or tranquillity is being simple, direct, and uncomplicated. The state of being of nowness has no extra attachments, and therefore it is peaceful. Peace is like a rock simply sitting on the ground. In the state of peace, you don't need to make an inventory: "Now I am feeling my toes; now I am feeling my ears, my temple, my shoulders, my heart." You simply feel your body as a whole. Body is sitting there on the ground, and you are that body.

In discussing meditation, sometimes we talk about the psychosomatic body, which is made up of both the somatic part, the body, and the psychological or mental part, the mind. Your mind and your body are sitting together. In meditation, it isn't important to sort out which part is mind and which part is body. Really, what difference does it make? The point is that, altogether, life is experiential. If you don't have an *experience* of life, you don't have life. As long as you are not a corpse, you have experience. You might experience life as 75 percent pleasurable and 25 percent painful, or the other way around. Those percentages are not purely abstract measurements; they are in reference to your *experience* of pain and pleasure.

You may draw logical or "objective" conclusions from your experience, to prove that you exist or that things exist independent of your imagination or your mind. That may be the scientific approach. However, scientific observations are also experiential. In order to have an observation, there has to be an observer or at least an observing of something, which is an experience.

In meditation, we work directly with our experience, without having to draw conclusions. When your body sits, you have that experience of body sitting. Don't complicate it more than necessary. Bodily sensations come and they go. You don't do anything with them. As questions arise about our experiences in meditation, this approach is to see those questions as thought patterns, or thinking. In the practice of meditation, you label everything that happens in your state of mind as discursive thought. You say to yourself, "This is thought, this is thought, this is thought, this is thought." No matter what arises, everything is labeled as thinking.

Regarding everything as a thought pattern is quite demanding. It requires a certain amount of bravery, or heroism. When you take the approach that everything is thinking, you begin to realize that right and wrong, good and bad, safe and not safe, actually don't exist. Therefore, it is also a very freeing experience. So regard whatever arises in meditation as thinking. Let the thoughts pass through. "Easy come, easy go" could be our motto.

In your practice, you will have many experiences of body. You may imagine that there is a big hole underneath the ground, so the ground could collapse at any moment. You worry that you might find yourself in a dark pit. Or you may feel the solidity of the earth that you are sitting on. You may feel as though you were sitting on crystal rock, which can't be penetrated and has never been explored. Even if you're very shy or afraid, you can't dig a hole to hide in, because you are seated on solid crystal rock.

So many experiences arise when we practice. They are all relevant. We can't just say that such experiences are neurotic. For that matter, we can't say that they are expressions of sanity, either. Such experiences are just experiences. Our experience is real, true, and direct. Appreciating that is the best way to begin.

Sitting in a chair or on a meditation cushion, feeling your body and experiencing your breathing: This experience is yours to appreciate. You just sit there, experiencing your form, your atmosphere, experiencing a sense of life, purpose, time, and temperature. The unnecessary complications should be simplified into one-pointedness. Appreciating your experience in this simple way is the development of peace, which is the starting point in the practice of meditation.

12

Life Force

The basic point of mindfulness is to be completely, totally in touch with what happens in your body and the environment around you. You are not reduced to an inanimate clod of earth while you are meditating. You may feel your pulse or your heartbeat. You feel your breathing. You hear sounds and see sights. You feel the temperature around your body. You feel vividly that you are alive.

Surprisingly, this experience is often reinforced when we have physical difficulties. They trigger a survival mechanism in the body that can make you feel very alive. If you are meditating while you have a fever or the flu, you may feel wretched, and you may wonder why you bother to practice meditation at all when you're ill. You may find, however, that meditating in the midst of physical discomfort actually helps you to be in your body, and it may help you to connect with the aliveness or the living quality of your practice. Similarly, when you have pain in your joints while you're sitting, in your legs, your knees, your back, or your neck, those sensations provoke awareness.

The experience of pain may remind you of the possibility of death. We know that we usually get sick before we die. So sickness or any kind of physical weakness or unpleasant sensations in the body may trigger an almost automatic warning system. You might be dying! When you're sick or injured, people may treat you as if you're quite pathetic, even if you just have a splinter in your thumb. Your friend might say to you, "Poor thing!" Somebody rushes to pull the splinter out with tweezers, as though he were saving you from death. Any chaos that comes up in your life may remind you of your inevitably approaching demise. However, when you feel concern or even panic in reaction to sickness, it also triggers a feeling of life. It awakens your life force and inspires you to push back. You try to reestablish your feeling of well-being or balance. Particularly in the practice of meditation, discomfort can increase an appreciation of being alive.

In fact, the fear of death can only be experienced in relationship to the appreciation of life. An unpleasant feeling that reminds you of death also reminds you of the preciousness of life. In the sitting practice of meditation, when you feel an ache in your body, which makes you feel crummy, it may also inspire you or fuel your practice. So there is a sympathetic interchange between pain and pleasure here.

When you are in pain, something in you takes over and drives you to survive. That's the life force. In fact, you are not all that delicate. You are somewhat tough. You have the force of life within you. Obstacles may evoke the force of death, and there is a constant struggle between the two. But there's a lot of vigor in that interplay. When you feel affected by pain, when your legs hurt while you are meditating, for example, a certain vitality comes out of trying to compensate for the pain. Working with this interplay in the practice of meditation is working with the life force, which is also referred to as the mindfulness of life.

Sometimes, physical discomfort in meditation goes beyond one focal point and becomes generalized. You may feel as if a powerful sickness were being transmitted from the earth through your body. Your entire body hurts. You feel the pain in the base of your body, your seat, and then this painful irritation comes up your spine, your arms and your legs, until it reaches your head and even your eyelids. This is just one of the natural—and somewhat unpleasant—ways in which we experience pain and discomfort. At the same time, this experience evokes a powerful sense of life. It's like holding a hot cup of tea and feeling the heat being transmitted from the teacup through your hand. It's as though you can feel the magic of reality transmitting the heat. It's very real and personal. When you feel the heat, you might be afraid of getting burned. You may worry that you might spill the tea on your chest or in your lap. Should you hold on or should you let go? If you panic and let go, you'll spill the tea, but if you hold on more tightly, the cup might get so hot that you will also drop it and spill the tea all over yourself. It's an uncertain situation.

The sensations of being alive may be threatening and a bit confusing, and we may develop a powerful reaction or survival instinct in relationship to them. We might prefer to ignore them, but if we ignore the reality of pain and pleasure as part of life, then when we encounter difficulties or more extreme situations, we panic much more. That's when we spill our cup of tea.

So from the beginning, our approach to working with sensations should be direct, simple, and literal. In the practice of meditation, we don't try to gain a pleasurable state of happiness by ignoring pain, nor for that matter are we deliberately seeking pain or trying to punish ourselves. We are just being mindful of whatever arises.

Although things should be down to earth in our practice, this is not to say that there is no inspiration there. We can be genuinely inspired by being with the earth, with the body, with the trees, the rocks, the grasses, the water. Inspiration also comes from being with the highway, with the traffic lights, being with your father, your mother, a policeman, your doctor, or even your lawyer.

Those everyday experiences are usually regarded as somewhat mundane and unimportant. If you are seeking a transcendent experience in meditation, then daily life may seem too ordinary to associate with. You may think to yourself, "I am above all this." By doing so, you cut yourself off from the magic of reality and from what I would call basic sanity, the basic experience of things as they are. Instead, you are developing a personal dreamworld.

The antidote is to have more contact and connection with the earth, by realizing and cultivating the life force, the power of being alive. You have a pair of eyes, a nose, ears, mouth, arms, and legs: you have this thing called a body. People refer to you by a name: Jack or Jill, Michael, Judy, or Joe. That is you, whether you like it or not. The more we drift away from this thing called our body, our basic existence, the more problems we have.

Maybe we feel that we're confused. Therefore, we try to get away from our confusion. Then we become more confused, trying to get away from the confusion of the confusion. It's endless. Running away from one confusion after another creates a chain reaction, endless echoes. Finally, you find yourself nowhere, painfully nowhere. It can be completely claustrophobic, like being trapped in the nest of a black widow spider.

One morning while I was preparing to teach a seminar on mindfulness, I stepped out of a little trailer in the mountains where I was staying, to sit on the porch and look around. I had a beautiful view of the hills in the distance, and I could see a big tent in the valley where people were practicing meditation. I said to myself, "How beautiful this place is—so many beautiful clouds and trees and greenery. There is the tent where people are meditating. It's fantastic, ideal—a perfect world!"

But then . . . a message arrived that someone was coming up to the trailer to talk business with me. That beautiful world suddenly didn't exist anymore. It had shrunk up into a concept of feeling hassled. The clouds and the trees were still there. Everything in my ideal setting was still there, but somehow they didn't exist for me anymore. They'd been reduced to irritation and timing, programming and scheduling.

After a little while of being in that irritated frame of mind, I found myself smiling at myself, as I reflected on my upcoming talk that evening. I realized that, since I was going to talk about life force and the mindfulness of life, the message I had received was the best possible one. My dreamy level of appreciating nature was brought down to the ordinary level where one has to relate with one's schedule. That was the best possibility of all.

You can't hover in your dreams forever. Eventually, you are going to be brought down to earth. I realized that it was my duty to keep to my schedule. There was no choice. People had arrived for the seminar. I couldn't kick them out or ignore them.

Sometimes, the truth of life makes us indignant. We feel that we deserve more happiness, less hassle, or whatever it is that we want. So we complain about our life. But in the midst of that complaining process, we find that we are suddenly quite connected to reality, quite sane. In the midst of enormous bundles of insanity, there's a sudden realization of sanity. We have to face facts, simply and precisely. That is what we're talking about in terms of the mindfulness of life. It is the experience of being alive, which can happen in the midst of irritation or chaos.

When there is more chaos, we have a tendency to check back with ourselves, to be sure we're coping okay with the chaos. The process of checking back or checking in with ourselves connects us with immediate reality. It's good to do this: Just check in, without any purpose. The checking in is a kind of jerk. When you check in and evaluate the whole thing, the situation may seem extremely messy. You may find some leaks in your pipes. But just check in. Just look, look, look, constantly.

This checking-in process is part of the practice of meditation. When you meditate, you may find a lot of chaos in your thoughts and feelings, as well as conflict, uncertainty, and a feeling of being a fool. At the same time, you begin to hear sounds more clearly, you begin to see more clearly, and you begin to feel your body more distinctly. When you check in with this process, you realize that there is a feeling of being very alive in the midst of all this chaotic activity. You also begin to recognize that this feeling of being so alive is connected with being sane, being fully there. If you check in again and again, then slowly, slowly, you connect with sanity. Sanity in this case is being in contact with reality at its fullest, as much as possible. It is being fully mindful, to begin with, and beyond that, there might be a greater experience of freedom.

Feeling your life force is an experience of being. It brings your mind into focus, into one-pointedness. You may wonder if it's really this simple, or you may feel that you've learned a new trick. In fact, it is the first trick and the last trick at the same time. It runs throughout the practice of meditation, from top to bottom, beginning to end.

When you meditate, you actually are meditating even when you think you're not. You have no choice, in fact. In your mind, you may be miles away from your meditation cushion, but you're still sitting there. There is still communication between your body and your mind. It might seem like a schizophrenic level of communication to be aware of both the irritations of your body and your distant thoughts. However, you are having a real experience of life, a real experience of reality, whether you like it or not. There is some magic, if you'd like to put it that way, some force of life that takes place. It doesn't matter whether you have an enormous pornographic show going on in your mind or whether you are having a delicious mental meal miles from the meditation hall. In actual fact, you are still sitting on your meditation cushion or in your chair. If you check in with yourself, you'll realize this.

When you have a lot of mental distraction, it is very helpful and necessary to relate with the breath. The awareness of your breathing accentuates that you are sitting on the cushion. Breathing is also a powerful symbol of being alive. If you stop breathing, you are dead, so experiencing breath is experiencing life, constantly. When you mentally lose track of where you are, that's precisely the point where you need the discipline of following your breath. Then, as you begin to notice that you are breathing, it brings you back to the aches and pains in your body. You are actually alive and struggling.

There is a connection to your life, some sanity that truly takes place when you meditate. Sitting on a cushion or in a chair and practicing meditation is more than a token gesture. It is an expression of commitment, an expression of truth, honesty, and genuineness. That commitment is the basic aliveness in our practice.

There is so much speed in our society. We have so many things to do. We jump back and forth from one thing to another. The practice of meditation teaches you to slow down and appreciate your life. Appreciate your partner's cooking. Appreciate your kids. Appreciate your job. Appreciate the weather. Experience everything in its own way.

When you drink hot tea, it burns your lips and your tongue. That's reality. There's a good lesson: how to drink tea. Everything in life is literal, direct, and personal—and very demanding. But that demand seems to be necessary. Your commitment is to be present. You're going to experience life as it is, rather than your expectations from the past or your desires for the future. You're going to relate with life in the fullest sense.

13

Spontaneous Discipline

Spontaneity is the expression of directness and fearlessness, in both the sitting practice of meditation and in life altogether. It is taking continual delight in our life, by connecting with the first fresh thought, which is present in every moment. Spontaneity also brings freedom from physical and psychological tension. When the energy of wanting to let go and the energy of wanting to hold on are in conflict, it produces tension. Spontaneity is an expression of nonaggression and a celebration of what you are, so it is not connected with push and pull or give and take. It is the expression of humor, joy, and delight.

Although spontaneity opens the doors to freedom, a truly spontaneous approach can't take place without discipline. We might think that there is a contradiction between the two, but in fact, spontaneity and discipline go together. Spontaneity itself is possible because you are *there*—which is the discipline. The discipline of being in the present relates not just to the practice of sitting meditation alone but also to our general life situation, our experience throughout the day. Joy and humor in everyday life come from being fully there.

Sometimes when we're disorganized or don't plan ahead, we say that we have a problem with being too spontaneous, and that we need to be more disciplined. However, discipline is not a remedy you apply after the fact. It works hand in hand with spontaneity right from the beginning. When you feel delighted, resourceful, or open, you experience those spontaneous qualities because you're already being disciplined. Otherwise, you couldn't actually connect with them. They would be like slippery goo gliding through your hands, too slippery to catch. Discipline doesn't hold you back; it actually allows you to make the connection with spontaneity.

Spontaneity and discipline also work together in the creation of art. Artists have made many attempts to fight against or emerge from established tradition to make a totally new statement. Trying to escape from the means, or the media, is very difficult. But the attitude behind the creation of a work of art can be spontaneous and direct. For example, the brushstrokes used in Asian schools of brush painting and calligraphy are part of established traditions, but each painting is unique.

I believe that aspiring artists should be trained in an almost orthodox conservative way so that they incorporate the technical knowledge and the wisdom of the traditions they are working within. This also applies to meditation and contemplative training. At the beginning, your training should involve strict discipline. Later, you should feel that you can afford to open yourself and express yourself freely. Spontaneity is possible in part because of the exertion and the discipline you have experienced. Then, spontaneity will also have a sharp eye. It will be clear seeing, which is the expression of discipline.

Applying direct exertion brings you back to square one, to the first thought level. You work with what is there simply and directly. Real spontaneity allows everything to be out in the open. You are not shielding yourself from the sore points. There is nothing to play games with anymore.

When we first practice meditation, we don't begin "properly." We begin as we *are*. We may even begin in a somewhat distorted or confused way. Having no idea how to begin properly, you begin somehow or other. You just do it. People are often bothered by this haphazard way of beginning. They are looking for perfection right from the start. But there is no such thing. You have to start on the spot with the confusion and the imperfection. Spontaneity begins with the clumsiness, the imperfection, by making a fool of oneself. Let us be fools; let us do it.

Our primitive way of beginning, whether it is in our sitting practice or the application of awareness practice in everyday life, is the first glimpse we may have of spontaneity. From the beginning, it needs to be linked with exertion. Having discovered the practice of meditation, if we hope to gain something from our practice, we need to make a commitment to continue, to stick with the practice. Exertion is becoming acquainted with and becoming accustomed to working hard. It provides the routine discipline that we need in our practice and in our lives.

Most of the challenges and the questions that we face in life are about communication, honesty, and our skill in working with situations. Focusing on possibilities for some higher attainment or transcendence can be a hindrance and a distraction in meditation and in life. We become more self-conscious, and we start to second-guess ourselves. We can't let ourselves be proper fools. Then we are stuck in the middle, not being wise and not being fools. We need a more direct approach that helps us with the down-to-earth problems and challenges in our lives.

Demands of all kinds arise in life, and we may have to deal with successive seeming dead ends. Problems often appear to be unsolvable. They manifest as obstacles, as a thick wall in our way, and we don't know how to go beyond the wall. The wall always has an opening, but sometimes the doorstep in front of it appears to be very high, and we have to decide whether to climb over it or whether to try to avoid the problem altogether. Sometimes we'd rather peer through a hole in the wall rather than having to go through it. But it is necessary to step over the doorstep and walk through.

Often even pleasurable situations are reminders of a mental or emotional blockage or difficulty. You might be enjoying yourself at a restaurant with a friend, but it reminds you of the difficult day facing you at work tomorrow. Rather than trying to smooth things over or trying to ignore what's coming tomorrow, exertion is directly becoming acquainted with the problems after problems that come up.

In our practice and in our life, working with all the challenges is an ongoing journey, not just a one-shot deal. When we meditate over a long period of time and make a commitment to meditation as an ongoing part of our life, we discover that meditation provides us with a path to work with the obstacles that present themselves. We could speak of walking on the path of meditation. This is taking a lifelong journey through the obstacles and the challenges that arise. In fact, the path is made out of obstacles.

The path exists because of what we don't know as well as what we already know. If you want to go to New York City, you take the journey to New York because you are *not* there. Otherwise, it would be unnecessary and redundant. But because you are not there, therefore you go on this journey. You have no idea what will happen once you get there. Still, you are inspired to make the trip. You usually don't know exactly what the goal is, but you keep going.

As you walk on the path, at the beginning your vision may be clouded, but still you are seeing *something,* which encourages you to keep going. Then, as you go along, you start to see certain aspects of your experience quite clearly. So you can look at your journey in both ways: you are ignorant, so you go on a journey to become better informed. On the other hand, some existing intelligence or insight inspires you to make the journey in the first place.

Experiencing physical or psychological weakness in yourself is an obstacle that frequently arises on the path. Sometimes, you feel that you have run out of resources—you don't have enough energy to take another step. That experience is like running out of gasoline on the road. Or you may have a feeling of being a helpless child calling for his mommy. You feel so confused. The way to deal with feeling weak is to just *be* with it. Just be weak. Then you will begin to regenerate energy. In fact, when you let yourself be weak, you start to appreciate that some energy is already there. You realize that your weakness is very energetic.

In fact, one doesn't have to put out that much effort. One just has to be open, and then the reference points, the effort or the energy, will come to you. You acknowledge the effort and go with it, rather than working yourself up, or cranking yourself into high gear.

You may view your practice as overcoming obstacles that appear on the path, or you may regard the obstacles themselves as the path. Perhaps this is a subtle distinction, but it's an important one. Experiencing physical and psychological blockages in your practice is discovering the textures of the path. Sometimes, the road is smooth and covered with asphalt; sometimes it's rocky and strewn with boulders; sometimes it's a dirt track through the forest. You should try to follow the path rather than destroy it. In fact, if you want to have a path to follow, it has to be made out of something! So you've got to have those problems. They are not particularly regarded as bad or good. They simply bring you down to earth, so that you feel that you are actually there, rather than drifting up among the clouds.

We've talked a great deal about just letting yourself be, but in fact, when you encounter doubt or a blockage on the path, some exertion is required. You have to exert yourself to let go.

We often think there's a conflict between exertion and just letting ourselves be there. However, exertion *is* letting yourself be there, in this case. To experience openness and letting things be, you yourself have to let go, which is the exertion part. Freedom—the spontaneity we've been discussing—is the outcome of taking a leap. You have to push yourself to leap into freedom.

The language here could be problematic. Exerting or pushing yourself to let go doesn't imply being aggressive. Aggression would be pushing against something to get what you want. In this case, when we push, we are not getting anything back. Rather, we find ourselves having leapt and being freed, but we can't even hold on to that. You can't freeze yourself in midair. Try it.

The leap we're talking about here is not deliberately pushing yourself on an extreme physical or mental level. Rather, it's your attitude. You take the attitude that a potential leap is available. Then the opportunity will actually approach you, so that you can let go, still with a certain amount of exertion. It's as though you are walking along a path, and then you find that there's no more ground ahead of you. You arrive at an enormous cliff. You've lost your ground, and the only way to proceed is to leap, to go along with the groundlessness. I'm not speaking literally, but metaphorically or psychologically, of course. I wouldn't recommend actually jumping off a cliff.

In working with obstacles on the path of mindfulness, outside feedback is not always that helpful. It's often better to rely on the internal feedback from your struggle or obstacles. Our own efforts in our practice and in our life show us the path. We certainly don't need to get outside advice too often. Rather, we can work with our immediate experience. There is a pattern to our experience; there is a texture to our path. There is a style in which the energies begin to flow by themselves, so there is constant feedback built into our experience, which is quite apparent and obvious. So you don't need to be dependent on a parental or authority figure.

When you ask yourself a question about your practice, you often find that the answer is already available to you, if you really look into the situation. Rather than checking with someone else for confirmation, you should be willing to stick your neck out, relying on your own impetus and insight. We do this all the time. We stick our necks out, we take chances, but then we pretend that we're not doing so. If we feel that we have the safe, reliable security of relying on our parents, a teacher, or another authority figure, we pretend to be helpless and wretched in order to get their help. But as soon as we are out of their sight, we stick our necks out again anyway. Everybody involved knows what's going on, so we might as well admit it to ourselves.

The adviser in your life will often give you the same advice that you can provide to yourself. The fluctuations of life are always there, situations are always there, your experience is always there, and you will find that there are predictable or obvious patterns. Instead of being preoccupied with asking somebody else to confirm what this is all about, you might rely on your own experience. The purpose of a good teacher in any case is that he or she will push you back on yourself, to square one.

From this point of view the practice of mindfulness is particularly designed for people who practice meditation on their own. Some people live in remote areas, where contact with a meditation instructor or teacher is limited, and only limited contact with fellow meditators is possible. This approach is also aimed at people who are consumed and challenged by their domestic lives and may be under financial, career, and family pressures. They don't always have a lot of time to attend meditation programs. The practice of mindfulness is applicable precisely when there are constant demands in your life. You might be working in an office, a restaurant, or a factory, or you might be a college professor. Mindfulness can be applied in all the many occupations that exist in the world.

The practice of meditation is geared for lonely people—and everybody's a lonely person, from this point of view. As soon as your umbilical cord was cut, you were alone. As you began to grow up and dissociate yourself from your mother and father, you grew into a lonely person. The more poetic or maybe polite way of saying loneliness is "aloneness," I suppose, but actually the two words are pointing to the same thing. Loneliness is both an attitude that we can cultivate and a given fact of the human situation. If you can accept that it is part of life, loneliness can be a source of some solace. You find that you can keep company with your loneliness.

It is quite amazing that there is human wisdom that addresses our loneliness. Human beings have been so kind to us, the lonely people. Someone actually came up with the practice of meditation, which is very kind, and remarkable of them. It is fundamentally what is called compassion.

It is necessary to work with these areas of loneliness, exertion, spontaneity, and discipline in our lives. These aspects of our experience can provide a very *real* path, because these experiences are connected with everyday life and its challenges, and the mindful approach is designed for that life.

14

Touching the Surface of Mind

Another foundation of mindfulness practice is being mindful of the mind itself. This is not as mysterious as it may at first sound. Mind reflects our thoughts, feelings, sensations, and emotions, which is its experiential or experience-based aspect. Gaps, or glimpses of clarity without any particular content, also appear in our minds. I refer to these as the intuitive aspect of the mind. These glimpses are just part of our basic makeup, rather than being particularly insightful.

We experience both aspects of mind—the experience-based aspect and the intuitive glimpses—in the practice of meditation. It may be somewhat challenging to sort out how to relate to these two qualities in our practice. We may wonder whether we should focus on the experiential or the intuitive aspects of our minds. Should we pay attention to the mental and emotional upsurges or to the momentary clarity without content? This can be a source of restlessness in the practice of meditation. We are unable to decide which of these to rest with.

In the sitting practice of meditation, thoughts and emotions come in the form of memories, habitual thought patterns, fantasies, and expectations for the future. This experiential aspect of our minds is quite provocative and entertaining, and it is an easy source of preoccupation. The intuitive aspect, or the clarity, is refreshing and provides relief from the torrent of thoughts and emotions. The emotional reference points in our minds change from one topic to another, and they also alternate with this sense of relief. We experience the gears shifting from one mood to another. Occasional clarity occurs between one mood or fantasy and the next.

We ask ourselves whether we should pull back from those preoccupations and try to be a good boy or girl, clean and pure. However, sometimes our boredom suggests to us that we might enjoy these little entertainments. If we can involve ourselves in fantasies of this and that in our practice, it almost provides a break from the tension of sitting. Sometimes we feel hypnotized by our memories, and we find that we can kill time this way. Three minutes go by, five minutes go by, or maybe even ten minutes go by. When we indulge in this way, we feel both some satisfaction and a sense of guilt at the same time.

Is there a conflict between the emotional and mental content and the occasional gap? Which should we focus on? When you experience mental confusion and emotional cloudiness, you might hesitate to come back to the awareness of the breath. You might like to remain there exploring, finding out about the emotional cloudiness. In fact, you can relate to both of these situations: the empty clarity and the emotional and mental content. In working with the mindfulness of mind, you don't need to choose one or the other.

The intensity of our conflicting emotions is a workable situation, and it is also a source of developing our mindfulness. Without some juicy material to work on, as we discussed in the previous chapter, there's no journey. The practice of meditation consists of working mindfully with those conflicting thoughts and emotions as well as with the occasional gaps that may create a feeling of relief. Without those two, there is actually no meditation. I think people often have the wrong concept of meditation, thinking that once you become a professional meditator, you won't have to think a single thought. The only activity will just be to b-r-e-a-t-h-e. But that could be quite zombie-like, quite horrific. You utilize the conflicting emotions; you don't cut them off. You may cut through the hard core of ego. But the emotions are just the tentacles, which could be pickled!*

So the technique of mindfulness of mind is to be with whatever happens. The movement of breath, the experience of the body, and the fickleness of thoughts all take place simultaneously. Obviously, you don't stop breathing when you think. Mindfulness here is a larger notion of covering all the areas of breathing and the thought patterns.

Concentration usually implies that we have one focus rather than splitting our awareness between more than one object at a time. But in this case, at the level of mindfulness of mind, our concentration or overall awareness can develop a more panoramic quality. It's a beam of light that expands or widens when it reflects off an object. With our light beam of mindfulness, we touch the highlights of the emotions and the thoughts, we touch the highlights of the breath, and both are seen simultaneously by the mindfulness of mind. You may hear sounds; you may see visions and sights of all kinds; you may have thought patterns of all kinds. All of those are connected by a binding factor, which is the mind. Therefore, whenever there is mind, there are possibilities of being aware of whatever is happening, rather than reducing the focus of our concentration to one level alone. Overall, this is what we mean by mindfulness

---

* Spoiler alert. Don't read this footnote if you want to work out the wordplay for yourself. It seems, to this editor, that the author is saying that our emotions can be preserved (pickled), rather than eliminated. He appears to be making a wordplay on the idea of pickling. Pickles are also called preserves.

of mind, where the cognitive mind is actually functioning in its utter precision.

Awareness of the glimpses of clarity in the mind is also direct and simple. When mind is preoccupied with an emotional theme that involves you personally, you are very taken up with those preoccupations that arise. In contrast to those thoughts there are gaps, which don't make a big deal about *you*. The gap is just a change or a shift. It's like transferring the weight from your right leg to your left leg. When that transfer is taking place, there's a gap where the weight isn't exactly on either foot. It is not particularly mystical. It is just a shift, a change of emphasis. That gap in our meditation is also touched by the presence of awareness.

The totality of the mindfulness of mind is like sunlight simultaneously reflecting on both the mountain peaks and the valleys. Such awareness isn't regarded as a big deal, as such. You don't constantly refer back and tell yourself, "I'm being *aware* now." "Now, I'm being *fully* mindful." Nevertheless, a quality of being there takes place, which goes along with a quality of what could be called "touching." One touches the thoughts. One touches the emotions. One touches the gaps. An even distribution of mindfulness takes place, in that whatever one is touching, there is also the simultaneous experience of touching the other aspect, or the other shore.

You are gently touching everything throughout your state of mind. It's like stroking a kitty-cat. As your fingers move down the cat's back, you feel the individuality of each hair, but you also feel the continuity, the totality of the hair. This approach involves sharpness, precision, and simultaneous awareness of many different individual components. It's like looking at your toothbrush. You don't have the actual, literal, gross awareness of each bristle on the toothbrush. Yet you see all of those bristles, all of the toothbrush, completely, at once. Your mindfulness is direct and literal, but at the same time it is panoramic.

There is total awareness without being selective. You might

find this idea of mindfulness rather perplexing, and you might ask what being mindful really means in this context. Are we still talking about being fully committed to the very moment? In the practice of the mindfulness of mind, if you try to be selective and find *the* famous experience of mindfulness, as you look harder and harder, you begin to lose the sense of mindfulness altogether. There seems to be no such thing as real mindfulness at all. The whole thing becomes illusory. You find yourself peeling away the layers of the onion. You think you are being mindful, but you are *watching* yourself being mindful. Then you're watching yourself watching yourself being mindful. And then you're watching yourself doing all that. There's a constant, constant, constant reflection back and forth, and finally you get completely bewildered. At that point you may have to give up the idea of developing or cultivating "true" mindfulness as such. You just accept what goes on and make the best of it, so to speak. In this way, you leave the world undisturbed, rather than trying to disentangle everything too efficiently.

This approach, from one point of view, is not at all demanding. It's a light touch rather than hard work. From another point of view it is *extremely* demanding. If you put all of your effort and energy into something, it occupies your mind, which makes you feel better. However, if your mindfulness practice is touching and experiencing everything without being heavy-handed, you feel suspended in the middle of nowhere. It seems very dubious. You may feel that there is more to go, more to develop in your practice. You may feel that you've only done something in a halfhearted way rather than being fully engaged. But you are there, constantly, at the same time, without any aggression.

If we push ourselves to the level of enormous concentration, if we try to push ourselves painfully and exert ourselves more than is necessary, it becomes aggressive rather than meditative. Meditation practice, however, is regarded as the action of nonaggression, which is a light touch.

Nonaggression is quite different from an absence of conflict. When you look from the meditative or mindful point of view, you see how even conflict can contain nonaggression. You might discover how the rugged desert of conflicts in your life could be quite still, quite peaceful. Cactuses are sticking up with thorns growing out of them, but those seeming threats are very earthy.

It's difficult to explain this logically. However, it's possible that the ups and downs we experience can in themselves become the evenness or equanimity of our experience. They can actually be a symbol of peace. The textures of conflict are not gentle, smooth, nor particularly soft. But *how* the challenges exist and how they present themselves is more important than the texture. Seeing in this way is precisely the meaning of mindfulness. You learn to look from an existential point of view—allowing things to exist—rather than trying to even them out or bulldoze the whole landscape. With this view, fighting or resistance isn't necessary.

It is possible to glide through the different landscapes of mind without becoming distracted or wooly-minded, because there is an actual experience of each moment. You develop enormous appreciation of the little things that happen in everyday life. Life becomes humorous and workable. Sound, sight, feelings, and experience altogether become *real*. Then, you never tire of looking at the same rock sitting outside your door. Each time you see it, it's refreshing.

If you paid less attention to what is happening, you might become dreamy. Things might become vague. In this case, however, there is actual contact, actual touch. You are touching the surface of mind very gently. At the beginning, it doesn't seem like a particularly heavy dose of mindfulness. However, in the long run, as you go on, this light touch makes a big impression on your mind.

15

Recollection

The practice of mindfulness meditation is beginning from the beginning, using body, breath, and mind as the mediums for our practice. These are the only mediums that are available to us in this world, on this planet. One purpose of meditation is to develop a feeling of stillness and solidity in one's practice. In order to become more open, one needs to establish the ground from which one will open. From the simplicity of mindfulness we begin to develop clear seeing, and we begin to make a transition to insight meditation. We are attempting to prepare ourselves for a path that is dedicated to working with other people as well as ourselves. The first step in that direction is to work with our awareness in post-meditation, our everyday awareness or mindfulness in action, as well as in the formal practice of meditation.

This term, post-meditation, is used to remind us that meditation is a reference point in everyday life. The sitting practice of meditation is the starting point for developing mindfulness. It establishes a reference point for awareness of yourself as well as a general awareness of your environment and your experience as a whole. From the general pattern of basic awareness in your practice, you step out and expand yourself into everyday life, using the mindfulness you develop in meditation as the starting point for mindfulness throughout life. Meditation is the source or the basic inspiration, and from there, slowly, mindfulness and awareness begin to emerge in your life as a whole.

At some point you may begin to realize that there is very little difference between sitting and not sitting. The idea is that the practitioner of meditation should eventually develop a fuzzy boundary between meditation and post-meditation. In that way, there is continuity, which is the continuity of mindfulness, or the precision of one's practice, throughout one's life.

The basic post-meditation practice is to cultivate glimpses of awareness in everyday life. The approach of post-meditation or mindfulness in action is not so much trying to re-create the meditative state of awareness in everyday life, but it is reflecting back on the awareness you experience in mindfulness meditation. You might wonder how to reflect back and what you reflect back on. It's rather vague at the beginning. One has to try it and see what happens.

The recollection of awareness throughout the day is an unconditional experience. By that we mean that it's a sudden glimpse of something that doesn't have a description. It's not a certain, particular experience that you remember, but simply remembering to be aware, so this practice is called the practice of recollection. Awareness does exist, and the memory or the recollection of that awareness acts as a reminder. From that memory a jerk takes place, a very short glimpse, in a microsecond.

When you have that glimpse, you might want to hold on to it or possess it and try to inquisitively investigate it. Holding on is not advisable, because then you might try to create artificial awareness based on reinforcing a watcher or self-consciousness— which is not what we're trying to encourage. This experience of recollection can't be captured. We can't even sustain it. In fact, you should disown it. So, first there is recollection; then you disown this glimpse; and then you just continue whatever you are doing—cooking or brushing your teeth or driving your car. You don't have to be startled or unsettled by the glimpse.

Sometimes there is some slight recollection that is hardly noticeable. Some awareness happens, but you may think it is just your imagination. You think that probably nothing is happening at all. It doesn't really matter whether something is happening or not. You're not trying to document your awareness. You are trying to practice it.

The practice of recollection may seem like an insignificant thing to do. You might wonder what it does for you. In our lives, the chain reaction of our mental processes and the network of our habitual reactions often create a whirlpool of confusion. We are not just subject to or living in this whirlpool at this moment; we are also manufacturing confusion for the future. We keep generating a chain reaction of confusion because we think that it provides us with security for the next minute, the next month, the next year. We want to make sure that there is something to hang on to.

It's quite amazing that we manage to manufacture our own future confusion using our present experiences of hanging on to neurosis. With our present actions and attitudes we create the seeds that blossom in the future. The present situation is inescapable. You are somewhat settled or habituated to it, so you don't want to do something different in the future. You don't want to have to change gears. Generally people enjoy living in the world of confusion because it is much more entertaining. Even suffering itself is entertaining in a strange way. Therefore, we create further neurotic security over and over again on that ground. Although we may complain and we suffer, we also feel quite satisfied with our lives. We've chosen our own self-existence.

The practice of recollecting awareness throughout the day is the main way that we can prevent ourselves from sowing these further seeds of habitual cause and effect. In the present moment we can disrupt these chain reactions. The memory or recollection of awareness creates a gap. Earlier we talked about the gap between one mood and another. Here we are talking about another kind of gap: awareness that can cut through the continuity of our struggle to survive. The practice of recollecting our awareness shortens the life of that fixation. And that seems to be one of the basic but powerful points of meditation practice.

With meditation we don't reject the present situation. Beyond that, the application of awareness is the way to sabotage confusion's hold on the future. Awareness is a simple matter. It just happens. You don't have to analyze it, justify it, or try to understand it. In the midst of enormous chaos, recollection is a simple action. There may be problems, but you can simplify the situation rather than focusing on the problems. Natural gaps in our experience are there all the time.

Our post-meditation experiences will be clouded with all kinds of ups and downs. Sometimes there is a sense of enormous excitement. You feel that you are actually making some progress, whatever that is! Sometimes you feel that you are regressing and that everything is going wrong. And then there are neutral periods where nothing happens and things are somewhat flat. Those signs of progress or regression are just temporary meditative experiences, which occur both in the practice of meditation and in our daily awareness practice.

Sometimes people worry that their practice is actually regressing, but that never happens. Sometimes, if you push yourself too hard, your ambition will begin to slow down the speed of your journey. But as long as meditation is not conjuring up something imaginary, there aren't any problems with regression. You can't fail at practicing meditation. You would have to give up your mind, and you can't do that. Meditation practice is a haunting experience. Once you begin, you can't give up. The more you try to give up, the more spontaneous openness comes to you. It's a very powerful thing.

Often, having practiced mindfulness for a while, people

describe temporary meditative experiences of pleasure or joy, emptiness, and clarity, which is sometimes called luminosity. It's as though light is finally being cast on your life. These three experiences—emptiness, clarity, and joy—are not regarded as extraordinary signs of progress. They are simply experiences or phases in your practice. When these experiences arise, you just go on practicing and cultivating the continual practice of awareness. What you work on is checking your basic awareness, cultivating that jerk of awareness.

You don't have to have complete comprehension of what awareness is all about in order to experience a glimpse of awareness. It may feel like a very primitive glimpse, but that's why it's workable in some sense. In fact, recollection is almost a memory of bewilderment, which brings a jerk of awareness and puts you back to square one each time it happens. You don't work on awareness like collecting a paycheck and putting the money in the bank. Rather, you have the awareness, and then you disown it.

If one is open to these glimpses and to the possibility that they might recur, they come much more frequently. The effort of the discipline here is not so much direct or deliberate effort but rather that you are accommodating possibilities of recollection. This effort doesn't save you from the chaos of a given day. It is a much more long-term approach.

The recollection of awareness throughout our lives is the preparation for beginning to help others. Initially we are purely working on ourselves in order to develop mindfulness and awareness. When you have developed some stability within yourself, there are possibilities of working with other people and dealing with many situations. Our ability to help other people is largely based on our ability to sabotage the self-centered background of our own lives, through the development of mindfulness and awareness. When our orientation is less self-centered, wisdom and skillful means, or skillful action, will begin to appear.

You might think that terms such as *wisdom* or *skillful means* sound either very advanced or quite abstract, but they are completely present, immediate possibilities, not something that might happen to you one day in the future. Wisdom and skillful action are possible even at this point. It's not truth as a myth of the future, but the truth of the living situation.

Part Three

Mindfulness in Action

16

Touch and Go

At this point in our discussion I'd like to introduce some further instructions for the practice of meditation. These instructions could be especially useful in relation to the discussion of working with the emotions in this section of the book. The touch-and-go instructions were first introduced to be used by people attending a month-long practice retreat or a three-month practice and study retreat, so these instructions are attuned to issues that arise in the intensive practice of meditation. However, they are also applicable to daily practice and they help us in working with our daily lives, or mindfulness in action.

Attitude

As we've already discussed, in the practice of meditation there is an attitude that brings about possibilities of mindfulness. This attitude is not a matter of forming an opinion. Rather, it is directly cultivating the awareness of mind, which is precisely what mindfulness is. You are aware that your mind is aware of yourself. In other words, you're aware that you're aware. You are not a machine; you are an individual person relating to what's happening around you.

Touch and Go

We could use the phrase "touch and go" to describe the cultivation of mindfulness and awareness. Mindfulness in this case is being mindful of the sense of being. The *touch* part is that you are in contact, you're touching the experience of being there, actually being there, and then you let *go*. This approach applies to awareness of your breath in the practice of meditation, and it also applies to awareness in your day-to-day living situation.

In the practice of meditation, touch and go works with how we directly *feel* our experience. The idea of *touch* is that you feel a quality of existence; you feel that you are who you are. When you sit down to meditate in a chair or on a cushion, you *feel* that you are sitting on your seat and that you actually exist. You are there, you are sitting, you are there, you are sitting. That's the *touch* part. The *go* part is that you are there, and then you don't hang on to it. You don't sustain your sense of being, but you let go of it.

With touch and go, there's a feeling of individuality, a feeling of yourself as a person. We are here; we exist. We feel this, directly and simply. Then, we let go, which is a sense of carelessness, of not feeling too much concern.

Working with Emotions

Then, there is a further *touch* that is necessary, which applies not only to awareness of a sense of being but also to the mindfulness of emotional states of mind. That is, one's mental state of aggression, lust, or whatever you are feeling has to be acknowledged. Those states should not just be acknowledged and then pushed off. You should actually look at them. This is an important point. There should be no suppression or shying away. You have the experience of being utterly aggressive and angry, or being utterly lustful, envious, jealous, or whatever you feel. You don't just say, "Oh, it's okay. This is what's happening." Or, very politely, "Hi. Nice seeing you again. You are okay. Good-bye, I want to get back to my breath." That is like meeting an old friend on a train platform, someone you haven't seen in a while, who reminds you of the past, and saying to him or her, "Well, excuse me, I have to catch the train to make my next appointment." That attitude is somewhat deceptive.

In this approach to practice, you don't just sign off. You acknowledge what's happening in your state of mind, and then you *look at it* as well. The point is that you don't give yourself an easy time so that you can escape the embarrassing and unpleasant moments, the self-conscious moments of your life. Such moments might arise as memories of the past or the painful experience of the present. Or you may feel the pain of future prospects, what you're going to do after this. All those thoughts and feelings happen, and you experience them, you look at them, and only then do you come back to your breath.

This is extremely important to do. Otherwise, there is the possibility that we could twist the logic all around. If you feel that sitting and meditating, coming back to the breath, is a way of avoiding problems, that *is* the problem. You might feel your practice is extremely kosher, good, sensible, and real, and you don't have to pay attention to all those little embarrassments that happen around your life. You can regard them as unimportant and just come back to the breath. If you do this you are creating a patchwork; you are bottling up problems and keeping them as your family heirloom. Instead, it is important to look at those embarrassments and only then to come back to breath. And even then, after you have looked at them, there's no implication that, if you look at them, it's going to free you and provide an escape from one painful point to another, or that it's the end of the story.

In fact, most of the problems in life do not arise because you are an aggressive or lustful person. The greatest problem is that you want to bottle those things up and put them aside or patch over them, and you have become an expert in deception. That is the biggest problem. Meditation practice is supposed to uncover any attempts to develop a subtle, sophisticated, deceptive approach. It is designed to uncover those patches.

Working with the Breath

The attitude toward breathing in meditation is also related to working with touch and go. Once you are set properly in your posture, you begin to naturally focus on the breath going out of you. As the breath is going out, become the breathing. Try to identify with the breath, rather than watching it. This is the *touch* part. You are the breath; the breath is you. Breath comes out of your mouth and nostrils, goes out, and then dissolves into the atmosphere, into the space. You touch that process; you put a certain energy and effort toward that.

Then, as you breathe in, you boycott your breath; you boycott your concentration on the breath. That is the *go* part. As your breath goes out, let it dissolve. Then, just abandon it; boycott it. So breathing in is just space. Physically, biologically, one does breathe in, obviously, but you don't make a big deal of it.

Then another breath goes out—be with it. So the process is: out, dissolve, gap; out, dissolve, gap. It's constant opening, abandoning, boycotting. In this context *boycotting* is a significant word. If you hold on to your breath, you are holding on to yourself. Once you begin to boycott the end of the outbreath, it's as though there were no you and no world left, except that the next outbreath reminds you to tune in. So you tune in, dissolve, tune in, dissolve, tune in, dissolve. This is another way of saying touch and go, touch and go, touch and go.

Labeling Thoughts

As we know, many thoughts arise in the midst of practice. "Well, back at home, what are they doing?" "When should I do my homework?" "What should I write about next?" "What should I paint?" "What's happening with my investments?" "I hate that guy who was so terrible to me." "I would like to make love." "What's the story with my parents?" All kinds of thoughts arise naturally. If you have lots of time to sit, endless thoughts occur.

We have already talked about labeling thoughts as part of the practice of meditation. It is a very simple technique: we reduce everything to thinking. Having discussed relating to the emotions in terms of touch and go, we should address the importance of also labeling emotions as thinking. Usually if you have low-level mental chatter, you are willing to label this as thought. But if you have deeply involved emotional chatter, or fights and struggles in your mind, you call those *emotions,* and you want to give them special prestige. Acknowledging emotional states of mind through the technique of touch and go does not mean that emotions deserve special privileges in our practice. We might say to ourselves, "I'm actually angry, it's *more* than my thought." "I feel so horny, it's *more* than my thought." That can easily become self-indulgence or a means of avoidance, a way of avoiding the realm of actual mind. In the practice of labeling our thoughts, it's important to view whatever arises as just thinking: you're thinking you're horny; you're thinking you're angry. As far as meditation practice is concerned, none of your thoughts are regarded as VIPs. You think, you sit; you think, you sit; you think, you sit. You have thoughts, you have thoughts about thoughts, and further thoughts about those thoughts. Call them thoughts. You are thinking, you are constantly thinking, nothing but thinking. Everything is included in the thinking process, the constant thinking process: thought, nothing but thoughts and thought patterns.

Walking Meditation

Up to this point we have been focusing entirely on the sitting practice of meditation. However, there is also a practice of walking meditation. If you take part in a group retreat, it's very likely that you will be introduced to walking meditation as a practice that you do between sessions of sitting meditation. You may also do walking meditation practice at home by yourself, between sessions of sitting meditation, when you want to practice for a longer period of time.

In group situations, sometimes people treat walking meditation as an opportunity for dramatic display, to compensate for the fact that when you sit, you can't do very much, whereas when you stand up and walk, you can at least exercise your self-existence. That is regarding walking meditation as comic relief, a time to do something extraordinary, or self-exploratory, self-expressive. That is not advisable.

Walking practice is still practice. Instead of paying attention to your breath, you work with the movement of your legs and the overall awareness of walking. Your body still has good posture. You raise your right leg, taking a small step forward. Then you touch the sole of your foot to the floor, and then your toes. Then the left leg takes a step: your heel presses down, then the ball of your foot touches the ground, and then your toes; then the right leg steps forward again, and it continues like that. It's a very natural, ordinary walk.

Your eyes are open while you're walking, of course, but generally you lower your gaze, rather than looking up or looking around at everything. Usually, during walking meditation, you are moving in a circle with other people around the room. Sometimes people walk quickly, almost racing relative to everybody else, or a person may walk *very* slowly. So you have to maintain an awareness of those in front of you and behind you.

In walking meditation you fold your arms at the level of your belly, with the right hand over the left. You tuck the fingers of your left hand in, making a fist around your thumb, and the fingers of your right hand cover your left fist. So your arms aren't just swinging or hanging at your sides.

Walking practice relates to your everyday life situation much more closely than sitting practice. It involves movement, and it is a transition from the sitting practice of meditation to what will happen at the end of meditation, when you rise from your meditation cushion and begin to move into walking in the street, speaking, working, and so on. So walking practice is an important link to post-meditation and mindfulness in action. However, it's still part of formal practice. Regarding it that way, as part of your mindfulness practice rather than as a break, you have to pay heed to it. You can do it somewhat deliberately but at the same time freely.

Group Retreat
Awareness between Sessions of Sitting

If you plan to do a group retreat for an entire day or over a period of several days or more, you may have questions about how to handle yourself during the periods when you are not sitting. Should you just tiptoe around as if you were walking on eggs, still trying to hold on to your meditation experience? Or should you make a big splash in your interactions with people? Or should you be somewhat dumb and hesitant and try to play along with other people's energy? You will undoubtedly be given instructions for how to behave between meditation sessions. You may be asked to observe silence. Even when silent, however, you are still interacting with others and responding to situations. The point is not so much that you should tiptoe, or make a big splash, or be hesitant. Instead, you should try to recollect the sense of meditational awareness that has developed in your state of being; just continue that way. This doesn't mean especially working with the breath or working with your walking during the breaks, but there is a *flash* of awareness, the *memory* that you sat. This was discussed in the chapter "Recollection."

Also, remember your commitment to this particular course, this retreat. You have set your intention in being here. The attitude is not particularly moralistic or a question of behaving like good boys and good girls. It's a basic recollection of why you are here. And you *are* here; you have sat and meditated; it's simple and factual.

Another general recommendation for group retreat situations—one that I strongly recommend, as a matter of fact—is to minimize unnecessary chatter. This means you should refrain from conversing or commenting among yourselves. You limit your verbal statements to what is purely functional and necessary. For example, one might say, "Pass the salt," or "Close the door." Of course, you may be doing your retreat in complete silence. Functional talking is a kind of middle ground between that and just chattering away. It can be more challenging than silence, because you have to decide what is functional!

Another challenging aspect of a group retreat is the mealtimes, even if they're conducted in silence. Mealtimes, I have observed, are often seen as a moment of release, a moment of freedom—which is unnecessary. I think we can approach this differently. One problem during meals can be unnecessary chatter, but even if that is not taking place, there can be a quality of meals as time off, a gap, a vacation. You are eating and drinking—no doubt having a relatively pleasant time—and you regard it as completely outside of what you are doing in the meditation hall. There's a dichotomy, a shockingly big contrast, which is unnecessary. If you cultivate such an approach during the mealtimes or during personal time—thinking that this is your free time, your time to release energy—then obviously your sitting practice is going to feel like imprisonment. You are creating your own jail.

You might feel that the meditation hall is where serious practice takes place, and when you get out the door, everything's free, back to normality or something like that. The physical environment may be somewhat isolated and restricted in a retreat setting, but you still may feel that you can indulge in your own free style during your personal time and proclaim your individuality in some way, even if you do so silently. By doing that, you might develop a negative reaction toward the meditation hall, considering it a jail, while the other places, away from practice, come to represent freedom and having a good time.

The suggestion here is that we could even out the whole thing and have a good time all over the place. *This* is not so much a jail, and *that* is not so much a vacation, freedom, a holiday. Everything should be evened out. That is the basic approach: if you sit, if you stand, if you eat, if you walk—whatever you do is all part of the same good old world. You are carrying your world with you in any case. You cannot cut your world into different slices and put them into different pigeonholes.

We don't have to be so poverty-stricken about our life. We don't have to try to get a little chocolate chip from just one part of our life. All the rest will be sour, but here I can take a dip in pleasure! If your body is hot and you dip your finger in ice water, it feels good. In actual fact, it's painful at the same time, not completely pleasurable. If you really know the meaning of pleasure in the total sense, this dip in pleasure is a further punishment and an unnecessary trick that we play on ourselves.

In sum, the practice of meditation is not so much about a hypothetical attainment of enlightenment as it is about leading a good life. In order to learn how to lead a good life, a spotless life, we need continual awareness that relates directly and simply with life.

17

Meditation and the Fourth Moment

Mindfulness is a process of growth and maturing that happens gradually rather than suddenly. You may celebrate your birthday on a particular day, but this doesn't mean that you suddenly go from being two years old to being three when you blow your candles out at your party. In growing up, there is a process of evolution and development. Meditation practice is a similar evolutionary process, one that takes place within you in accordance with your life situation.

There is continuity in the journey. You begin solidly, you progress solidly, and you evolve solidly. Don't expect magic on the meditation cushion. The idea of a sudden magical "zap" is purely mythical.

In reality, nothing can save us from a state of chaos or confusion unless we have acknowledged it and actually experienced it. Otherwise, even though we may be in the midst of chaos, we don't even notice it, although we are subject to it. On the path of meditation, the first real glimpse of our confusion and the general chaos is when we begin to feel uncomfortable.

We feel that something is a nuisance. Something is bugging us constantly.

What is that? Eventually we discover that *we* are the nuisance. We begin to see ourselves being a nuisance to ourselves when we uncover all kinds of thought problems, emotional hang-ups, and physical problems in meditation. Before we work with anyone else, we have to deal with being a nuisance to ourselves. We have to pull ourselves together. We might get angry with ourselves, saying, "I could do better than this. What's wrong with me? I seem to be getting worse. I'm going backward." We might get angry with the whole world, including ourselves. Everything, the entire universe, becomes the expression of total insult. We have to relate to that experience rather than rejecting it. If you hope to be helpful to others, first you have to work with yourself.

The first step, as you certainly know by this time, is to make friends with yourself. That is almost the motto of mindfulness experience. Making friends with yourself means accepting and acknowledging yourself. You work with subconscious gossip, fantasies, dreams—everything that comes up in your mind. And everything that you learn about yourself you bring back to the simple awareness of your body, your breath, and your thoughts.

Beginning to make friends with yourself brings relief and excitement. However, you should be careful not to get overly excited about your accomplishment. If last night's homework assignment was done well, it doesn't mean that you are finished with school. You are still a schoolboy or a schoolgirl. You have to come back to class, you have to work with your teacher, and you have to do more homework, precisely because you were successful. You have more work to do.

You begin to experience a greater sense of fundamental awareness. Such awareness acknowledges the boundaries of non-awareness, the boundaries of wandering mind. You begin to realize the boundary and the contrast. Your mindfulness is taking place, and your confusion, your mindlessness, is also taking place. You see both, but you don't make a big deal about it. You accept the whole situation as part of the basic overall awareness.

Not only are you mindful of your breath, your posture, and your thought process, you are also fundamentally aware. There is a quality of totality. You are aware of the room; you are aware of the rug; you are aware of your meditation cushion; you are aware of what color hair you have; you are aware of what you did earlier that day. You are constantly aware of such things.

Beyond that there is a nonverbal, nonconceptual awareness, an awareness that doesn't rely on facts and figures. You discover a fundamental, somewhat abstract level of awareness and of being. There is a feeling that "This is taking place. Something is happening right here." A sense of being—experience without words, without terms, without concepts, and without visualization—takes place. It is unnamable. We can't call it "consciousness" exactly, because consciousness implies that you are evaluating or conscious of sensory inputs. We can't even really call it "awareness," which could be misunderstood. It's not simply awareness. It's a state of being. Being what? It is just being without any qualification. Are you being Jack? Are you being Jill? Are you being Smith? One never knows.

This may sound rather vague, but the experience is not as vague as all that. You experience a powerful energy, a shock, the electricity of being pulled back into the present constantly: here, here, here. It's happening. It's really taking place.

There is an interesting dichotomy in this situation. On the one hand, we don't know what it's all about. On the other hand, there is enormous precision, directness, and understanding. That is the state of fundamental awareness, or insight. You begin to see inside your mind on the level of nonverbal awareness. Nonverbal cognitive mind is functioning. You may say, "Now I hear the traffic; now I hear the cuckoo clock. Now I hear my wristwatch ticking. Now I hear my boss yelling at me." But you also have to say, "I hear, but I don't hear at the same time." Such totality is taking place. A very precise something or other is happening. That is the ultimate state of awareness. It is nonverbal, nonconceptual, and very electric. It is neither ecstasy nor a state of dullness. Rather, a state of "here-ness" is taking place, which we have referred to earlier as nowness.

Nowness in this sense is very similar to the fourth moment, which was introduced in Chapter 8, "The Present Moment." This term, "the fourth moment," may sound more mystical than what is meant. You have the past, present, and future, which are the three moments. Then you have something else taking place, a gap in time, which is called the fourth moment. The fourth moment is not a far-out or extraordinary experience. It is a state of experience that doesn't even belong to now. It doesn't belong to what might be, either. It belongs to a non-category. We have to call it something, however. Thus, it is called the fourth moment. The fourth moment is the state of non-ego, going beyond the limitations of your habitual self. It is a very real experience, an overwhelming experience, in which nothing can be misunderstood. It is sometimes called the knowledge of egoless insight. The experience comes at you rather than you searching for it.

You are able to work with yourself and your life on the basis of that experience, through the constant reminders arising in everyday life, all your little daily hassles. You forgot to pay the telephone bill, and the message from the phone company is getting heavier and heavier. They are about to turn off your phone or sue you. Your motorcycle is about to catch fire, because you are over-revving the engine. Your grandmother is dying. Your family is demanding your attention. You can't afford to forget about them. All kinds of past and present reminders appear.

Many problematic situations or even a general state of turmoil may arise in your life. When you look closely at where the problems came from and what they are all about, you may begin to experience the fourth moment. Problems come and problems go, but still remain problematic. That may seem like a cryptic statement, but in that enigma you may encounter the fourth moment. Even when you appear to have solved it, a problem remains a problem. Nothing dissolves into a love-and-lighty beautiful creamy honey lotus lake. The problems remain potent, slightly painful, and sour—as if the world, the universe, were staring at you with a disapproving look. You haven't been quite as good or as wakeful as you should be. The world gives you that look of disapproval. When the sun shines, it looks at you. When the rooster cries cock-a-doodle-doo, it is saying the same thing. When someone's car honks, when the telephone rings, they are saying the same thing. There are ironic mockeries all over the place.

It is not that the devil is against you and trying to destroy you. It is not that some magicians have put a spell on you and are trying to get at you. Rather, the world is very powerfully in a subtle way trying to remind you to remember your fourth moment—*the* fourth moment.

That moment is the essence of insight and awareness. Experience becomes so real and precise that it transcends any reference point of any doctrine that you are practicing. Whether you are practicing mindfulness, Christianity, Buddhism, or psychology, you are practicing life. In fact, ironically, you find that you can't escape. You find that life is practicing you. It becomes so real and obvious.

Experiencing the fourth moment is quite important in the development of meditative awareness. At this point in your journey on the path of mindfulness, everything in your life begins to haunt you. Sometimes the haunting process takes the form of pleasurable confirmation. Sometimes it is painful and threatening. There is the feeling of a ghost haunting you all the time. You can't get rid of it; you can't even call someone to exorcise it. That state of insight and simultaneously of being haunted is the experience of the fourth moment.

You feel that you are sitting and camping on the razor's

edge, making campfires quite happily, yet knowing that you are on the razor's edge. You can't quite settle down and relax and build your campfire, yet you still stay on that point, on that spot.

That state of hauntedness is the state of ego, actually. Somebody in your internal mental family, some part of your being, is beginning to complain that they are getting uncomfortable messages. The awareness of the fourth moment cannot materialize unless there is that slight tinge of being haunted by your own egotism. The hauntedness of ego and the egoless insight work together. That is what creates our experience.

On the whole, we should regard our practice and our journey as experiential rather than as being based on programmed stages of development. At the moment you may be following a particular program of practice and study. You've made it to the first level, and now you want to progress to the second level, which begins on September 2. Although we do all kinds of things in that fashion, we should understand that in reality our experience isn't programmable in that way. Often students try to examine themselves so that they will know where they are on the path of meditation, but this doesn't seem to work. We have no way of knowing where we are in our practice or how we are doing on the path of mindfulness, as far as some standard evaluation is concerned. However, we do know that we started on a journey, that the journey is continuing, and that the journey takes time and requires real commitment to our individual experience.

Experience cannot happen unless both black and white, sweet and sour, work together. Otherwise, you are just absorbed into the sweet, or you are absorbed into the sour, and there is no experience. You have no way of working with yourself at all.

We should be a little circumspect, however, when we use the term *experience* to describe our journey on the path of meditation. Conventionally speaking, when you refer to a future experience, you have an idea and an expectation, some premonition of what the experience might be. Somebody tells you about it; you know roughly what it is and you prepare for it. You wait for that experience to come to you. When it does, you exert yourself to fully experience whatever arises. In this scenario, everything is quite predictable.

But the experience of the fourth moment is not a programmable experience at all. It is an unconditioned experience that comes from the unconscious mind. This underlying consciousness, or the unconscious, is an abstract state of mind, a state of literal thinking that doesn't have logic formulated yet. It is an ape instinct or a radar instinct. In fact, we don't know where this experience comes from. It just comes. There is no point in trying to track it back to a source. The fourth moment doesn't come from anywhere. It simply exists.

It is as if you are taking a cold shower, and suddenly hot burning water starts to come out of the showerhead. It is so instant and so real. For a moment, when the hot water first hits your body, you still think it's cold. Then you begin to feel that something is not quite right with that particular coldness. It begins to burn you. It is unprogrammed experience, where you simultaneously experience hot and cold water, each in its own individuality.

The present is the third moment. It has a sense of presence. You might say, "I can feel your presence." Or "I can feel the presence of the light when it's turned on. Now there is no darkness." The present provides security: you know where you are, right here. You keep your flashlight in your pocket. If you encounter darkness, you take out your flashlight and shine the light to show yourself where you are going. You feel enormous relief, created by that little spot of light in front of you.

The fourth moment, on the other hand, is a state of totality and total awareness that doesn't need reassurance. It is happening. It is there. You feel the totality. You perceive not only the beam of light from the flashlight but also the space all around you at the same time. The fourth moment is a much larger version of the present.

The experience of the fourth moment sharpens your intelligence. Without this experience of egoless insight, you may just accept things naïvely, and such naïveté may be the basis for self-deception. You turn on the cold shower, and you expect everything to be okay. Everything seems predictable. You are not prepared for any reminders. Then this little twist of hot water takes place. Whenever there is that kind of a reminder, it is part of the fourth moment. If there is a reminder, everything becomes very real. If you don't have any reminders, you are at the mercy of chaos and confusion. The sitting practice of meditation provides constant reminders, and that is why it is so important. It boils down to that.

18

The Sword in Your Heart

America, like many other parts of the world, suffers from excess. There are too many cars, discarded plastic containers, jet fuel, and other sources of pollution and waste. There are too many choices in the supermarket. We have so many brands and varieties to choose from that we can't decide which particular flavor of which kind of food we want to eat. So we buy too much, which creates further garbage, further pollution. The more passionately interested we are in every detail of every thing we might buy, the more choices we have, that much more junk we acquire. Then, all this "stuff" begins to make us claustrophobic. This applies to our psychology as much as to physical belongings. Having so many choices of this or that psychology or approach to self-improvement encourages us to jump from one approach to another. It can become self-destructive. We end up producing further neurosis rather than further sanity.

Our basic makeup is a conglomerate of mind and body. We are intelligent, methodical, logical, perceptive, intuitive, and emotional—with a touch of animal instinct thrown in. Sometimes human beings are referred to as beasts or creatures, but there is more to us than that, and therefore hope, promise, and salvation don't have to come from outside. They come from within ourselves.

This country has more than enough raw material to work with: information collected and collated, books written, conflicts generated, and problems identified. Now is the time for us to get back to the source, back to reality. That reality provides all kinds of clues, and all the clues encourage us to wake from our dreamworld. They bring us back to square one.

We have to look into what we are, who we are, and what we are doing, basically speaking. If we do not investigate our makeup, we could encounter many difficulties, misunderstandings, and blind corners. Before we can solve our problems, we have to introduce ourselves to the problems. Otherwise we might think we are doing something special, something good and even liberating, but we might find ourselves doing the reverse. When we have considered the problems and the possibilities, we will be in a much better position to commit ourselves to a discipline such as the practice of meditation, which can provide us with the backbone, or foundation, and the confidence for our journey.

Each one of us has particular aspects, unique characteristics. You might have a tendency toward passion, aggression, or ignorance, or other emotional styles. You might be turned on a lot of the time, or angry, or spaced out. None of those qualities is rejected; all are included as part of our investigation into who we are.

Most of the time we play at being stupid, exceedingly stupid. That stupidity manifests in a number of ways. When we don't want to hear or see the real truth, we close ourselves off and make ourselves deaf and dumb to situations. We play at being extraordinarily naïve, with no interest in exploring the sharp points in our world. We ignore any uncomfortable messages provided by the world. We become completely numb. On the other hand, sometimes we use our intellect to confuse the whole issue, which becomes another form of numbness.

Those habitual patterns are ways that we reject parts of ourselves and prevent ourselves from discovering inherent wisdom. Such wisdom could penetrate the shell that we usually create around ourselves. But it's very painful to actually tear away the shell, the skin that provides security and protects our sense of me-ness, I-ness. So we tend to close ourselves in as completely as we can.

We sometimes blame our reluctance to open ourselves on lack of experience: "I'm not learned enough"; "I don't have enough practice." But in fact our hesitation is usually based on an unwillingness to do the hard work of relating with ourselves. We find it too painful and unpleasant. We don't actually want to go through a process of unmasking.

We might call ourselves by a different name, put on different clothes, and even move to a different geographic or social environment, to totally shield ourselves from criticism or exposure. The necessary "unskinning" process is covered over and replaced by gigantic wishful thinking. We don't really want to give in, give up, be exposed, or become naked at all. Instead, we often add extra baggage. In the name of a self-exposé, in the name of nakedness, in the name of complete openness, in the name of selflessness or egolessness, we put on a suit of armor. We proclaim, "This is it; this is the way to make yourself naked." You pronounce your new suit of armor, your further mask, as your vision of what you should be.

Ever since we were separated or popped out from the fathomless, nonexistent, beginningless, endless *That,* the wholeness of being, we've been trying to create our suits of armor, our masks, and shields of all kinds. If we have enough bravado, we also strategize and collect suitable weapons so that we can defend ourselves if anybody tries to penetrate our defenses. We might kill someone on the spot if he or she is too nasty or comes too close to us.

Isn't this going a bit too far? Really. But who's kidding whom? How much can you actually kid yourself, your colleagues, and all the others, whoever they are? Such a self-deceptive approach not only affects us but also begins to affect our children, our parents, our spouses, relatives, and friends. Then we're all brewing this neurotic soup all the time. We may finally manage to achieve the ultimate neurosis. We might achieve a monumental world of neurosis, speed, craziness, aggression, passion, ignorance, and jealousy, in the name of peace, war, religion, education, government, the police force, the proletariat, students, schoolteachers, professors, poets, writers, and everyone else.

We can achieve a lot in the name of our deception. But no matter how beautiful the paintings may be, how fantastic the poetry may be; how smoothly your car runs; how economically successfully your household is functioning; how great the relationships may be with your parents, your wife, and your husband; and how beautifully educated your children may be, growing up like beautiful young flowers—something is still missing. Something doesn't quite click. Something is absent.

I'm not saying that what we do in this world in our social and economic setups is not worthwhile. Rather, I'm pointing to the style of our behavior when we don't want to open ourselves to others. We may introduce ourselves to each other as if we were good friends. We may fight with each other as if we were bad enemies. Nevertheless we don't manifest completely who we are and what we are. We don't fully reveal ourselves. We still want to preserve and protect ourselves from the big wound, the big heart, within us.

I once saw an exhibit of swords at the Japan Society in New York. It took a craftsman a year to make each one, and each was exquisitely beautiful. These works of art express the sharp, penetrating, and naked qualities of reality. That sharpness and directness are what is missing in our lives when we are afraid of ourselves. The artful dignity of a Japanese samurai sword also symbolizes how we can cut neurosis from within rather than striking an outer enemy.

Such a fantastic sword is in us *already* as our awake nature. We should be proud that we possess such embryonic swords in our hearts. A lot of the time, however, we're trying to make sure that the sword in our heart isn't disturbed. We don't want to wake it up. We're afraid to jump and walk, let alone leap, in case that sword might awaken and might cut through us, from inside out.

Our self-protective mechanism is really the expression of ego's mania. In the sense in which I'm using the word here, ego is not the actual heart of who we are but instead is the shield that surrounds the penetrating sword that exists in our heart. Since we don't want to awaken or reveal the sword, we develop all kinds of shielding, a whole process of covering it up.

We're also afraid of demands from the outside, anything that might get inside us and encourage our inner sword to come out. We're very careful not to hug anybody too intimately. We don't want to do anything that might bring out the sword in our heart. We've become afraid, cowardly, and deceptive, so fearful of our own sanity.

However, ultimately we can't get away from our own wisdom. The penetrating sharpness that exists within us is an irritation that can't be ignored. Because this beautiful sword exists, because such a sharp blade and fantastically tempered sword is already in our heart, we have to work hard to avoid noticing it.

We make a shield out of concrete, foam padding, newspapers, whatever we have, to make sure that this truth within us can't get out. We don't realize that if that truth were allowed to come out, there wouldn't be any problem with it at all. When you begin to realize how sharp and penetrating your intelligence is and how open you could be, it is such a revelation.

Once you begin to experience the truth, you don't find your habitual occupations that interesting anymore. We use them as entertainment, a way to kill time and reinforce our sense of survival. When we entertain ourselves, we don't have to expose ourselves completely. It would be messy, and we're somewhat afraid of that messiness.

As well, there is some arrogance that prevents you from opening up completely. If you let go of your self-centered watcher, you won't be able to see yourself becoming a fantastic person. What would be the fun of that? You tell yourself that, in the end, when you see how great you are, *then* you'll actually give up your self-centeredness. That's your story line, your theory, but the truth is that, if you feel you're becoming great, you'll want to hold on to that experience. Your egomania reinforces itself. It's like becoming a little dictator, a short-lived Hitler, Mussolini, Stalin, or Mao Tse-tung.

The alternative, which is called egolessness, doesn't actually mean having "less" ego as opposed to "more." We are talking about discovering the nonexistence of such a thing at all. What we usually call "me" or "myself" is just the padding we put around our heart. That padding has to be, not rejected, but pulled away or penetrated. Often we think of opening as something that results from an external force coming into us, making a slit in our skin, and finally opening up our heart. In this case, our heart opens from within.

However, opening is not automatic. There has to be a definite commitment to actually surrender, give, open up, and abandon the usual securities around us. That ongoing dedication to openness is an important part of the journey, or the path, of meditation. Sometimes you might waffle in your commitment, feeling that your goal or destination is unclear. You hope that if you just keep on going, you'll get somewhere. You'll achieve something worthwhile. In actuality, if you aren't willing to work on yourself and you don't have a desire to open and to shed your self-centered egotism, you are getting nowhere.

All the meditation instruction that is provided to you may be fantastic, wonderful. Nevertheless, it could be a waste of time. It's up to you. How you make your journey will determine whether you make junk out of a genuine treasure. You aren't going to be zapped or saved on the spot. If you take such an attitude, you won't get anywhere. This doesn't apply just to meditation. It's also true in the everyday world. If you are a businessperson who thinks you are going to be a millionaire tomorrow—you think you will be zapped into "millionaire-ship"— well, that does not often occur. If you are working on a difficult relationship with your parents, your husband, your wife, your boss, or your children, there is no sudden zap that will solve everything. You might hope for a breakthrough, so that tomorrow you can just relax and smile and everything will be all right. That's not going to work.

A sudden zap only works in your microwave oven. You put your food in, you zap it, and it gets cooked instantly. Even that requires preparation, however. You have to buy the food first. Then you can put it in the oven, but the result may not be all that exciting. Often, the dish tastes rather strange.

Similarly, in the realm of mindfulness and meditation you can't expect a transcendental microwave oven. No achievement happens all of a sudden. There is a process of growth, a gradual process of developing ourselves. The process is systematic. No one is going to save us on the spot. Our progress is up to us. We need to ask ourselves if we are willing to undergo the complete operation. Do we want the sword to come out of our heart, or not?

19

Galaxies of Stars, Grains of Sand

One of our greatest fears is the fear of losing our identity, our selves. We may associate the loss of self with mental instability or with dying and our fear of death. However, being less self-centered and discovering a more open state of being, one that isn't so rigidly defined, could be viewed as a very positive and sane development. On a very mundane level, we may experience a momentary unexpected gap in our story line or thought process. We might consider this a moment of freedom, but our usual response is to panic and try to cover up the fact that we've lost the thread. Our panic takes the form of bewilderment and confusion, which enable us to play deaf and dumb, ignoring what we've seen.

In meditation practice, people sometimes equate dwelling in bewilderment with a meditative state of being. They may confuse being spaced out with experiencing openness and relaxation. They may try to make bewilderment into a comfortable home or nest in their practice. We often have a tendency to try to solidify our confusion as the proof that we exist, not just in meditation but in many aspects of life. We try to maintain the solid sense of self because we mistakenly think that we can't function or thrive if we don't have a solid, self-centered ego. As we discussed in the previous chapter, this is mistaking the mask and the suit of armor that we're wearing for the real body, the real birthday suit.

At some point, in order to maintain ourselves, we may even decide to upgrade our armor, because the original patchwork is not doing a perfect job. Occasional glimpses of uncharted territory are getting through, which is disconcerting. So we look for a brand-new and improved stainless-steel suit of armor, beautifully painted, with an expressive lacquered mask. We may try to buy our armor wholesale, or we may have to pay a hefty price for it. We may be able to use mail order or get it at a spiritual supermarket. Sometimes we can even get our armor for free. But whether we pay for it or receive it as a personal gift, we are still purchasing a way to shield ourselves from our basic bewilderment about ourselves and our lives.

Then, we learn to incorporate that new armor into our lives, so that we can walk around in that suit and even fight in it. Our approach is like that of the medieval knights, whose armor was so cumbersome and heavy that they had to be cranked up onto their horses, and then their spears and swords were handed to them. Similarly, we try to protect our façade all the time, at any cost, in the name of religious, social, educational, technological, and domestic realities.

There are a number of aspects or stages in the development of this mistaken sense of self or ego. This development does not take place over time, like a baby growing up into an adult. We create all the complications almost simultaneously, all the time, over and over again. We solidify the fundamental basic deception into a patchwork suit, and then we layer on other patchworks immediately, one after another.

The first patchwork is connected with the panic that was already alluded to. It is based on our reaction to our basic bewilderment. Altogether, the construction of the false self, or the ego, is a response to feeling confused and lost. We want to find ourselves. We think that we can prove ourselves to ourselves. The truth is that we cannot say that we are one entity, one existence. Our individuality is really a heap or a pile of experiences. We are made out of experiences of achievement, disappointment, hope, fear, and millions and billions and trillions of other things. All these little fragments put together are what we call our self and our life. Our pride of self-existence or sense of being is by no means one entity. It is a heap, a pile of stuff. It has some similarities to a pile of garbage. When we refer to something as garbage, we are speaking not about one thing but about a collection of many different things that make up the garbage-ness. All these elements are collected and mixed with one another. As they decay, they become extremely smelly. What we call our selves or our ego is similarly an amalgam of many things put together.

So who we are and what we are is uncertain. We think we exist; we think our name is so and so; we think we have a soul or ego of some kind; but really we have no idea how and why and what is exactly the case. Logically we may be able to justify our existence in detail, but experientially, we are much more uncertain. This me, this seeming experiencer, seems to be experiencing its me-ness, this-ness. Something seems to be happening here. Something is cooking, as they say. This uncertainty and our attempts to secure ourselves in response to it make up the first aspect or layer of ego, which is a sense of form.

The creation of form here is like a blue cheese that is constantly fermenting, growing one mold on top of another, all the time. Because you don't really exist in the way that you think you do, you are constantly trying to secure your existence. You are like that blue cheese, which tries to maintain itself by continually growing more mold, until the mold consumes the cheese, which dissolves into nothingness, a pile of moldy dust. We are not one wholesome, whole entity at all. We are a collection of things, all of which are uncertain as to whether they exist or not. So every cell of this consciousness is defeating itself and uncertain about itself. It's a dream we unsuccessfully try to maintain. That is the basic quality of form: a fermenting blue cheese that eventually consumes itself.

Although the struggle is futile and illusory, we still fight for our existence, trying to gain our glory by existing. We may even try to implicate religion in our plot. The essential wisdom or truth of most great religions is basically egoless to begin with, but that can be twisted, not just individually but on a societal level as well. Societies may grow out of a particular religious outlook, and then the state may become the instrument to protect religion and persecute nonbelievers.

I'm not talking in terms of a particular tradition as ego-oriented, but I am speaking in terms of how egotism affects people's minds, affects them personally. I'm not saying that we should tear down the churches or knock down the idols. That approach won't work. If we are at all interested in a genuine contemplative or meditative journey, we can't start by attacking things from the outside. We have to start from within. We need to look at where something went wrong or where something went right. We have to start from the inside, which is our mind, our consciousness, our state of being.

We may ask ourselves, how on earth did we get ourselves into this mess? And *who* did it? Whom can we blame? Who made the first big mistake? Who's responsible? You may ask these questions, but I don't think you'll find a single individual who made a gigantic enormous mistake. You might be tempted to blame organized religion. You could blame Christ; you could blame Muhammad; you could blame Moses; you could blame Buddha. However, trying to place blame distracts us from understanding how we got into this mess. Just between us, I'll tell you a secret: the problem came from being unable to relate to *ourselves*. Christ is here within us, and Moses is here, and Buddha and Muhammad are here, too. They're all here. We might be able to think of several hundred key religious figures and other paragons of human wisdom, and from some point of view, every one of them is in your head. Neither am I saying that religion is the answer nor that we should blame religion or tradition for our human predicament. We can't avoid the real issues by placing the blame on history, psychology, politics, or religion, and then turn to meditation as a clean and pure alternative. More to the point: Whatever we're into, if we say that it's the only way, the only promise, it's very suspicious.

The development of our confused self or ego that I'm describing here is related to this sense of feeling out our lives, trying to find out who is for us and against us, who is to blame and who or what will save us. You try to *feel* the sense of tradition, *feel* the resentment, *feel* the confusion, *feel* how we can actually identify ourselves, our conceptualized ego, with some concept or security that we can latch on to.

So the first stage in ego's development is latching on to form, trying to create a home in our confusion and bewilderment. The second stage is feeling. Or we could call it a sense of touch. We try to feel out or reach out to touch, to determine who is on our side and who is against us.

If you are in your bedroom in the dark, and the electricity isn't working in your house, you try to find your way out of the room by using your hands to touch the walls and things around you. You feel your way out of the room, as though you were a blind person. When you're feeling your way in the dark, you're trying to avoid running into things, and you want to find the door. If there is a big column, a sharp corner, or a piece of furniture that you might bump into, you try to avoid it. You also want to avoid tripping over anything that might be in your way. You might try to find your way to the bathroom. You might try to reach the closest window, so that you can pull back the curtains and see the moon, or open the window and let some fresh air in. So there's a quality of feeling out whether things are for or against you, good or bad. This primitive sense of feeling your way around in the dark is like ego's primitive attempt to feel out the textures of life. Altogether, this nonentity called me, myself, and I is trying to create a bag or a container for itself. It is trying to survey and secure its territory.

The next aspect of this project is impulse. Having developed some rough relationship or connection with the phenomenal world, and knowing which textures are smooth, which are rough, and which are irrelevant, we have reactions to those things on a very primitive level. We have the impulse to respond to situations. Whatever message seems to be coming to us, we want to latch on to that information and secure it as a reinforcement of ourselves. Our impulsive response to situations is to draw them in, push them away, or ignore them. Whatever appears, we are ready to leap forward, leap back, or stand our ground.

Having developed a rough sense of form and some feeling for our world, and having developed an impulse to respond, or crudely communicate, now we reach a stage where we manage to put our feelings into categories. If you stayed in that dark house groping around for a long enough time, you would begin to form an idea of what was in the space. You know that there's a staircase down over there, so you won't go in that direction. There's a stone column in front of you, so you have to be careful not to bump into it. The window is in one direction, food is in the kitchen over there somewhere, and the bathroom is down the hall. So although we are basically completely blind, we still develop some sense of direction, almost as an animal instinct. That very basic sense of categorizing is the beginning of concept, which is the next stage in developing a solid sense of self. It is not the product of wisdom—it is just labeling and naming things, quite stupidly.

It's as though we had given birth to a son or a daughter. Realizing that we are the parents of this particular child, we look around and try to find a name for him or her. The first thing we see is a piece of rock, so we say, "Let's call him Rock."

Or if we see a spider, we say, "Let's call her Spider." We feel pretty good about that. We are making ourselves so smart out of our stupidity. This approach is devoid of any vision or dance. We're merely finding the most convenient label or name for our child. We don't want to do any research or think about it anymore. We're playing it extremely safe.

Then we might go beyond that crude conceptual framework, trying to intellectualize the whole thing further. At this point, you develop further concepts, further reference points for what you are doing. "What happens if I fall down the stairs? I'll hurt myself." You refresh and embellish your concepts again and again. "If I run into a stone column, what will happen? I might hurt my forehead." We begin to put our feelings and impulses into more developed, almost scholarly, categories: "If I find my window, I get fresh air. If I get to the bathroom, I can relieve myself. And if I can find the kitchen, I can satisfy myself by eating food." Soon everything is neatly conceptualized.

The last process is what's known as consciousness. This is seemingly far from the fundamental bewilderment. Here, consciousness develops as a sense of totality and emotionality. We learn how to love and hate the whole process of our lives. "Those stairs are terrible. I hate them. And the column is bad, too. I don't like it because it might cause me to break my nose or bang my head and see stars. And that bathroom is good; it gives me relief. Food is fantastic; it will feed me, sustain me." So we begin to not just label things but to enshrine them as very good or very bad, for *me*! Although we possess all these faculties—our nose, our eyes and our ears, our body, our tongue and mouth, and our brain and our heart—still, basically we are not using them to see the world in a way that is clear, sharp, or unbiased. We are still playing blind, deaf, and dumb. We are essentially asleep. We may think we're having a good rest, a good sleep, but we're really operating out of a combination of self-indulgence, delusion, and horrific nightmares all put together.

We also develop further mechanisms within consciousness.

If we feel bored, we manufacture dreams of the past, expectations of the future, and a private cinema show. We can manufacture the illusion of a whole continuous scheme, which allows us to survive in this dark house, with the stairs, the column, the window, the bathroom, and the kitchen. We also generate subconscious gossip, as well as intense visual imagery and sensory experiences, quotations from the past, glimpses of past experiences, and future expectations all coming to us. The thought process acts as a screen, a thick shield to protect us. Finally, we not only have our heavy armor, but we have our whole castle secured; we have foot soldiers and subjects. We have become the king or queen, the ruler of the ego realm. We build a whole kingdom out of nothingness, which we call the world, actually.

Even after all this work, however, we still might find ourselves and our world disconcerting. We can't seem to put our finger on what is me, what is you. It all seems very uncertain. It's not because we are confused or stupid. Even the most intelligent and wise people couldn't figure this out. We all find ourselves lost in the piles of stuff that make up our experience of life. We feel completely lost much of the time, which is a true experience, in some sense. On the other hand, we could say that we were never lost because there was never anything to be found. The process of ego formation is like the constant churning out of galaxies and galaxies of stars, or grains of sand. Things are forming their own shape, dissolving, forming their shape and dissolving again. Recognizing that is the basic point of reviewing these stages or components of the self.

It's not that once upon a time there was the first bewilderment and now we exist on the fifth level of consciousness. The experience of a separate self or ego is a personal experience that happens all the time, constantly, in our state of being. Every moment has form, feeling, impulse, concept, and consciousness. That process is taking place on the spot, over and over again. This experience of our world is not bad. This is not about the Fall of Man, or anything like that. The stairs are not bad; the column is not bad; the bathroom and the dining room are not good. Those are just reference points we create. And without those, we can't actually experience anything at all. So they are necessary and important for us to relate to, in order to see how bewildered we are at this point. It's important to know and understand these facts of life, these patchworks.

The practice of meditation provides a way to work with this complicated experience of mind. In meditation, our attitude is not to label the self or ego as a villain or an evil force that needs to be destroyed. It is our stepping-stone. The only material we have to work with is our experience of ourselves, so it is our starting point. From this point of view, we should celebrate that we have ego. Therefore, we have some hope of discovering sanity.

20

The Fringe of Our Emotions

In this chapter we are going to talk about how to work with our emotions from both a narrow egotistical point of view and from a more open perspective. The characterization of ego here basically highlights its confused and self-centered side. As we have seen in the previous chapter, when we are trying to maintain the illusion of a fixed, permanent self, or ego, we occupy ourselves by constantly looking for new ways to prove the validity of its existence. One of our most powerful strategies is our involvement with emotional projections. We use aggression, passion, ignorance, and other confused manifestations of our emotions as ways to maintain our story lines about ourselves.

Building up these projections is like creating a sculpture of a dog and then deciding to dress it up. We make a costume for it. We put different clothes on the dog, based on whether we decide it's a boy or a girl dog, and whether we decide it's a priest dog or a fashion model dog. We dress it up, and then we gaze and gaze at it. Then, suddenly, to our surprise, the dog begins to move. Why, if *we* made this sculpture, should it be able to move on its own? It begins to haunt us. We created a naked dog, but then we decided to dress it up, which is laying further concepts or projections on it. To our surprise, our concept seems to take on a life of its own and begins to haunt us. You might say that's how we built New York City.

Sometimes our emotions produce dramatic upheavals. At other times, we feel quite calm, almost absent of any emotionality. However, no matter what is happening in our state of mind, ego wants to reinforce the undercurrent of the emotions flowing, because the energy of the emotions helps to fortify a bloated sense of self. To restate this: When we are filled with emotion, it seems that something, possibly something quite exciting, is happening and that there is a substantial entity at the center of the activity. When ego coopts the emotions in this way, they function like the limbs of ego's enlarged mental body, extending its reach and reinforcing its hold. Attaching the thought process to the emotions is the key here. Thoughts are employed as the veins and arteries that circulate the blood of ego through the limbs. Thoughts also function as the nervous system that carries impulsive messages back and forth from the limbs to central headquarters, the apparent heart and brain of ego.

Using thoughts in this way, ego hopes to become powerful and self-sufficient, generating its own energy, no longer needing to communicate or reach out to any foreign elements to maintain itself. Once this system is well established, then when there is an absence of emotional upheaval, ego generates its own dramas—so that even within a relatively calm state, fundamental panic and feelings of irritation and paranoia are generated, which cause us to initiate self-protective mechanisms. Ego's scheme is to appear constantly vulnerable to attack. When we feel this kind of vague vulnerability or anxiety, we guard ourselves and reinforce the whole area of ego. From ego's point of view, this is the ideal situation, creating a complete world that uses our thoughts and emotions to maintain our self-centeredness.

Meditation is a powerful tool to work with this pattern of projection. To cut through the efficient work of ego and dismantle the barriers it throws up to protect its central headquarters, we begin by working on the circulatory and the nervous systems of ego, that is, by working on the thought process. The complications and confusion of our thought process are there to ensure that ego's extremities, the conflicting emotions, remain securely connected to ego's heart and brain. If the efficiency of this system is disrupted and set into chaos, then it becomes easier to work directly on dismantling the fundamental structure of our egotism. By applying mindfulness, the basic technique of meditation, we bring the existing thought patterns into a simple situation, as opposed to the complicated one that ego has constructed. The practice we already have, the practice of meditation, undercuts ego's circulation system, its manipulation of the thought process. We do this by relating simply to posture, breathing, and labeling our thoughts.

We have many kinds of thoughts. There is the heavy-handedness of case-history thoughts. There are cunning foxlike thoughts and slippery fishlike thoughts, as well as grasshopperlike thoughts, leaping from one highlight to another. The way to work with all these aspects of our thought process is to simplify them into the basic practice.

This approach to meditation is not introspective or inwardly focused. If we try to work on ourselves by penetrating the depths or so-called deeper levels of thought, we may become introverted and we may intellectualize or complicate the whole process of meditation, rather than simplifying it. The tendency to centralize everything within ourselves by focusing on "me" and "my" and "my meditation" may be encouragement for the ego. It makes the ego feel that somebody is home, or somebody's at the office conducting business. This approach supports the illusion of centralized authority and efficiency within us.

To work with the problem of self-centeredness, the practice of meditation should get us out of the red tape of ego as much as possible. The basic practice is to relate with sitting, breathing, and walking from the point of view of awareness. This approach is outward facing. It is engaging our actual living situation. In the practice of meditation, physical sensations, movements, and our breathing all relate with the environment around us, the world outside. These aspects of our practice aren't purely focused within the body.

Centralizing energy inside the body is trying to hold on to the energy, which may increase tension and tightness. In the end, a person may begin to hate himself, because he hates the struggle that he's going through. In extreme cases, he may even want to destroy himself, to release himself from this internalized experience.

The alternative, stepping outside the ego, is boycotting the centralized idea of oneself. This approach is a refreshing process of opening by applying the principle of right mindfulness. This is not just ordinary mindfulness but mindfulness that is right on the spot. This applies not only to formal meditation practice but also to everyday life, to mindfulness in action. Here, mindfulness is complete identification or oneness with your technique and your activity. You don't try to be mindful, but you recognize that you are in a state of mindfulness already. It is a way of working with yourself in which you become one with whatever techniques you are using.

In our daily lives there are many routine tasks that involve repeating an action over and over again: swimming laps, stacking wood, vacuuming, washing dishes, brushing our teeth, shoveling snow, filing papers in a drawer or on your computer. Any repetitive, routine activity can be an aspect of our mindfulness practice. These activities provide opportunities to begin working with mindfulness in everyday life. Eventually, all activities can be part of the practice of mindfulness in action. This is not a replacement for formal practice, but our daily lives should also not be separate from mindfulness.

If you identify with the action that you are repeating over

and over again, it can be an experience of mindfulness. You can experience being absolutely right there, on the spot and being one with the action. It is the expression of right mindfulness in ordinary life.

Applying mindfulness in everyday life makes our experience much more spacious, and it also brings an awareness of the whole environment. That is the sign or hallmark of developing insight: starting to see the situation as a whole. If you are stacking wood, you are not only mindful of piling one log on top of another, but you are also aware of the whole woodpile and the space around it. If you're swimming in a lake, you have an awareness of the whole expanse of the water. There is greater awareness, as distinct from simple mindfulness. Mindfulness is primarily the aspect of the technique that is being right on the spot, and awareness is feeling the environment around that mindfulness. Awareness is more panoramic.

If you are watching the road too intently when you drive on the highway, you might miss your exit, because you're only paying attention to the road in front of you and you don't see the exit signs. You may be watching the car in front of you and the car behind you very mindfully, but if you're not aware of the bigger space, you might miss your exit. New drivers are often very cautious, paying a lot of attention to the speed limit and being very mindful of other cars on the road. When you first learn to drive, that may be a very good idea. Eventually, however, in addition to being mindful of the details, you also need an overall awareness as you drive.

If you purchase a new automobile, when you first drive it, you are very caught up in how the car accelerates, where the gearshift is, what all the lights on the dashboard mean, and other little details. But as you get to know your vehicle, you begin to tune in to the size of the car and how it operates, how easy it is to accelerate or to stop, and things like that. At a certain point it's as though your awareness becomes one with the car, so to speak. It's as if the car is your body. You are no longer calculating each movement, but you intuitively know how to handle your car, how to park it and drive it. You begin to feel as though the car is almost driving itself, rather than that you are driving the car. You feel that you are just making little adjustments to how it's driving. That's if you are a good driver. If you're a bad driver, then there will be lots of *you* involved in your driving.

In a similar way, in the practice of meditation, if you are tuned in to the environment, awareness or insight becomes part of your basic being, part of your ordinary behavior pattern. Awareness dictates to you, from that point of view. And at a certain point you may feel that you don't have to apply a technique in the formal practice of meditation. You almost feel as if meditation is conducting you rather than you are conducting the practice of meditation as such. You develop natural awareness as you start to relate to the total environment. This occurs as you become more acquainted with the practice and feel more relaxed with the breathing as well as other aspects of the technique.

The continuity of awareness links meditation practice with everyday life. Whether you're talking, eating, or walking—whatever you are doing takes place within a larger environment. With awareness, you recognize that you and your activities are all part of the environment. Connecting with the wholeness of the environment brings oneness with the action, making each activity more precise and direct. Then there's no room for ego's panic. You are able to cut the chaotic aspect of the thinking process, because at that point you are completely joined with the situation, not separate from what is there. That enables you to step out of the complicated thought process.

As this awareness expands, you also gain insight into your emotions. To begin with, you may only be able to approach the fringe of your emotions, not yet the heart of them. However, you are already able to see the emotions much more as they are, with their dynamic qualities and their simplicity as well. You also see that there is more to the emotions than just the intense highlights. You become aware of the larger emotional environment, realizing that the emotions have to function in a wider space. Anger and hatred come out of an environment of aggression. Passion and grasping come out of an environment of seduction. As you see this larger space, the emotions no longer have a cloudy, mysterious quality, but they are part of a living situation. Then, eventually, the emotions can be seen in their complete perfection—which is something we'll talk more about in the next chapter.

But to begin with, we should understand how meditation practice is a simple way of stepping out of the neurotic and chaotic aspects of the thought process. We can simplify everyday life, as well as bring simplicity to the sitting practice of meditation. Relating to both practice and daily life as fully as possible, being right on the dot in terms of technique, will bring us into an open situation where we don't have to guard against anything or concentrate on anything, either. We find that the meditative aspect of the situation is there already. That is the basic principle of how meditation allows us to step out of fundamental self-deception.

This approach is not cutting off the thought process altogether but is loosening it up. Thoughts become transparent and loose, so that they can pass through or float around in our minds more easily. Thoughts are often very heavy and sticky, and they hang around, demanding that we pay attention to them. But with this approach, the thought process becomes relaxed and fluid, fundamentally transparent.

In this way, we learn to *relate* to our thought process, rather than trying to attain a state without thoughts altogether. Thoughts have fundamental intelligence and energy to them, so you don't want to cut off the thought process. Rather, thoughts maintain their energy, but they become less solid and less irritating.

When our thoughts are less connected to maintaining egotistic self-centeredness, we appreciate life much more fully. Existence seems more colorful and beautiful. In terms of the projection of the dog that we started with, when you realize its nonexistence, you gain much greater appreciation for the real thing, the real dog.

It is like the difference between plastic and real flowers. Real flowers are much more beautiful, in part because of their impermanence. People appreciate the seasons, the autumn and the spring, because the seasons are a process of change. Each season is a precious time. In this way, impermanence is beauty.

We could also call this living quality nowness. Nowness is so fresh. It has nothing at all to do with the past or the future. It is absolutely pure, primevally pure. The present is right here.

21

The Heart of Emotion

There is no such thing as an ideal state of meditation. Awareness allows us to relate to our mental processes and to see the fundamental expression of mind as it is, including our thoughts. The meditator may find that many thoughts recur during the meditative state. These thoughts should be seen as waves on the ocean. They are part of our intelligence. When they aren't armed or heavy-handed anymore, they have a transparent quality. Thoughts also develop an evenness when we recognize that, fundamentally, nobody is trying to fight against anything.

From this experience we learn a different way of looking at life. Life is no longer warfare. Rather, it contains a quality of dance, and we develop an appreciation for its flowing process. With that basic attitude, we find that it's quite easy to relate to thoughts. Nothing is being conquered, and nothing has to be destroyed. Instead we develop a friendly attitude toward ourselves and toward our thought process. We realize that nothing has to be subdued or suppressed.

Seeing the transparent quality of things as they are brings

us into a new dimension of life. It also brings an absence of aggression and speed, so that finally we are able to fully enter into the territory of our emotions, both in their conflicted and in their pure state. We have discussed how the practice of meditation works with the thought process in dealing with the fringe of our emotional structure. The emotions are the basic mechanisms that trigger grasping or a battle mentality. Being friendly to ourselves, nothing has to be regarded as gain or loss, hope or fear, anymore. In our meditation practice, things are then easy and smooth, accompanied by a certain amount of discipline.

This also makes our projections less heavy-handed. Usually the projections tend to haunt us, and we feel that either we have to conquer them or we have to give in to them. That attitude is based on distrusting ourselves, not having a compassionate attitude toward ourselves. Often we think of compassion in terms of feeling sorry for someone or thinking that we are in a superior position to someone who needs our help. Here we are speaking of basic, fundamental compassion. The quality of this unconditional compassion is warmth and spaciousness. We don't have to push ourselves into extreme situations anymore, because we contain a spacious situation within ourselves. So nothing has to be pushed, and we can afford to let ourselves be.

This doesn't mean to say that a compassionate person will be very subdued and deliberate, speaking or acting slowly all the time. That kind of deliberate gentleness and slowness is a physical façade. It is not fundamental warmth and gentleness.

The discovery of compassion brings an understanding of the emotions as they are. The emotions become a decentralized process rather than a central force to maintain confusion. The emotions have their own space and their own creative process. When you realize this, you can actually become one with the emotions.

It's very tricky to talk about this. Becoming one with our emotions is not acting out or indulging in them, but it is connecting with the experiential quality of the emotions as they are. Trying to either subdue the emotions or put them into practice, by acting them out, is really two sides of the same coin. Both approaches are trying to escape from our real emotions, because we can't relate to them in their true nature. We think that we have to do something about them, either bottle them up or explode out with them. This is, as we've already discussed, largely based on not having enough faith or trust in ourselves—fundamentally not having a kind attitude toward ourselves.

The more intense our emotions, the more reason we have to get to the heart of the matter. However, we often feel that there is something terribly wrong with our feelings. For example, our anger may seem almost evil. There is something terrifying about it, which makes it seem impossible to relate to. We distrust ourselves. We think we might do something foolish if we allow ourselves to fully experience our anger. In fact, it's the opposite.

When we don't trust ourselves, we do random things to avoid our emotions. "Me" and "mine" and "my desires" or "my problems" seem outrageously overpowering. We feel that we have to do something about our feelings. However, when you are feeling angry, you don't have to act out your anger, say, by getting into a fight with someone. Nor do you have to suppress your anger, trying to forget it by going shopping for a new hat. There's another way, which is to actually relate to the bubble of energy that arises. This is connecting with an almost abstract quality of the emotions. By abstract, I mean the feeling that the emotions are almost an independent force, a primal energy. You relate to that simple, most basic quality of emotion, its abstract aspect, rather than getting involved in all the projections. You can almost see the visual, colorful aspects of your anger, the redness of it, the hotness of it. If you can experience that basic quality of emotion thoroughly, you begin to realize that it's not such a big deal anymore.

We don't see the emotions in their own true state because

we don't trust that we have the insight or the sensibility to relate to them that directly. Even if we have a sudden insight about how we might do so, we automatically seal off that thought, that possibility of understanding them.

The essence of the emotions is primordial wakefulness. That's a very powerful way of looking at them. We might think of mind as wakeful, as containing wakeful intelligence, but not the emotions, because we distrust them. We often see them as something overpowering, unnecessary or dreadful, something that we should cast off or find some way of getting rid of. But in fact, the basic nature of the emotions is that they are awake in themselves. They are like a snake curled to strike that unwinds itself in midair. That is the transcendental quality of the emotions, when we trust ourselves and we really enter into the emotions completely.

When we are not able to approach the emotions in their own true nature, they tend to cause all sorts of casualties, on the fringes of emotion. Emotional outbursts have a lot of speed or intensity. When they are spinning around, and when you just touch the fringe, you are pushed away, cast off.

The alternative is getting into the heart of emotion. For instance, the point of aggression is to arouse anger and hatred. If there is a "you" as a central person, a central reference point, your anger will overpower *you*. But if you become completely part of the anger, if you get into the is-ness of the anger, then anger's ability to overpower you disappears. There's no one there to overpower. Then anger becomes just a bundle of energy.

To take another example, the point of fear is to frighten you. If you become part of the fear completely, right in it, then fear has no one to frighten. So it's a question of absolutely getting into the heart of the matter.

Another way of seeing this is that you lose the concept of fringe and center altogether, in terms of your experience of your emotions or your identity as a whole. When you have a sense of being at the center, right in the middle or in command of an experience, you should regard the center as including the fringe of your experience as well. Sometimes you can only touch the fringe of an emotion or an experience, which might mean that something is threatening and you're trying to keep it at a distance. At that point, try to regard the fringe as also being right at the center. If the fringe becomes the center and the center becomes the fringe, there is no conflict between the two at all. There is no conflict within you or within your experience at that point. That is how the snake unwinds itself in midair. The emotions free themselves, rather than your trying to find a way to alter or destroy them.

We have to deal with the heart of the matter, the heart of situations. We have to work with both the cause and with the seeds of whatever develops in our life, rather than immediately jumping to conclusions. At the heart of the emotions we find emptiness, actually. When we realize that the forces at the fringe are also the center, we realize how much space there is. It is everywhere, all the time. And wherever there is space, space *is* the center in itself, as well as the fringe in itself, because there is no way to divide space into pieces. That realization breaks down the barrier of duality of "me" and "my projections" completely. There's no solid wall between us and our projections anymore. The wall between the two has been removed, because it never really existed. Finally we are able to perceive things without concept, without conceptualizing and judging, and without extreme emotional reactions. Things are seen as they are, because there's no fear of losing control of the center or control of the fringe. They have already been pacified or seen through.

This experience enables us to relate with other things in our everyday life. Whatever we perceive or experience in life is spacious, full, and complete when we don't have ulterior motives. If you don't perceive things with hunger anymore, your basic sense of poverty is removed. You trust things as they are.

This enables a person to act skillfully as well. Here, when we talk about skillful action, it's a question again of trusting in space, trusting the basic qualities of things as they are, rather than being skillful in creating or strategizing a particular outcome. Without ulterior motives, you can relate very accurately to situations. It's almost as though you yourself are a good speedometer that registers the speed of your vehicle or a good thermometer that registers the temperature of a situation accurately and precisely. You automatically become an accurate or skillful part of the process. From this point of view, if you are trying to be very clever by planning or reorganizing something, you are heading for complication and confusion.

Ignorance is refusing to accept things as they are, trying to impose a secondary meaning or trying to interpret things according to your wishes. When you artificially try to reinterpret something, your intelligence becomes feeble and freezes up. This frivolous intelligence binds itself, like a silkworm that binds itself with its own silk thread. You are creating your own bondage. When you see the absence of the barrier of duality, there is no room to be cunning or clever. There's no purpose to it, when things have been seen through thoroughly.

Rather, you begin to enjoy the details of your life as part of your path. When your journey is informed by meditative insight, then whatever happens in life becomes living insight. Situations themselves begin to act as reminders. They shake you, they slow you down, they warn you, or they may inspire you.

If we become more generous and open by removing the fundamental obstacle, or our façade, we are much more kind and loving to ourselves. Then our outside projections become kind to us as well. So the whole world becomes a loving world, one without aggressive conflict. Therefore, you discover that the world is filled with compassion. This inspires you to be friendly to others and to try to help them. You aren't trying to convert them to your ego. That approach doesn't apply anymore. Rather, because you see the other person's situation as it is, your chemistry and the other person's chemistry mingle together extremely well, absent any elements of aggression or passion.

I wouldn't call this an absolute state without extreme emotions. You could still have your emotional upheavals, but you also could have glimpses of openness. Those glimpses help you to become a more awake, open, and generous person. These glimpses of openness and generosity become the working basis, because they contain the qualities of compassion and skillful action. Then, each moment is a unique and beautiful opportunity to work on yourself. You don't want to miss the boat. Each moment is precious.

22

A Mindful Society

I did not come to North America to find a cozy home in the United States of America or because I appreciated elevators, aspirins, and all the other comforts available in this culture.* I came here initially and the teaching situation took shape because of people here. My arrival here was a response to an invitation, one that is becoming ever more powerful. It seems that this invitation might be extended indefinitely. Quite possibly, the practice of meditation and the appreciation of mindfulness will stay on this continent for a very long time—for generations and generations to come.

I wasn't invited here because something was missing. It's not as if any one approach alone presents the truth. Many contemplative and meditative disciplines are applicable and helpful. However, as the fundamental psychological confusion in this

---

* Chögyam Trungpa was born in Tibet. He arrived in North America in 1970. For more information about his life, and especially about the journey that brought him to America, please see A Short Biography of Chögyam Trungpa on page 185.

country has become heightened and thickened, increasing frustration, fear, and anger have developed. In particular, the American spiritual neurosis, both individual and group, has become, in some sense, a world monument. It deserves a gold medal. So, introducing disciplines for seeing the world in a very simple, ordinary, and basic way seems helpful and refreshing, and very much needed. That's why I came here, and that's why the meditative tradition of mindfulness is so appropriate for this country, as well as the rest of the Western Hemisphere.

People here have worked very diligently to develop themselves and to develop their country. People have achieved a lot in this populous country. Everything is supersized here, including the problems. To coincide with that, the award-winning neurosis of America deserves award-winning treatment.

Mindfulness in particular can address the problems generated by our individual ignorance and self-centeredness, which is what I have here called ego. To address this, we can use a personal means or discipline such as the practice of meditation. We can't blame this problem on anybody else. We might think that others made the mistake. However, our basic bewilderment is *ours*.

We would like to maintain this bewilderment. It becomes an occupation, one that we attempt to perpetuate. In truth, we can't maintain the confusion throughout our lives, twenty-four hours a day. At first, there seems to be a smooth pathway, but there are lots of gaps. There are big holes in the road that we might fall into, and we're afraid of those holes. We would like to have smooth living, with our neurosis operating seamlessly, simultaneously with our paranoia, all the time.

However, there is also interest on our part in understanding the meditative and contemplative disciplines that present alternatives to enshrining our confusion. These disciplines, which present a non-egotistical approach, are still fresh and new to us at this point. Until we have actually sat and practiced, however, we will never completely know the truth of what's happening in our heads and in our hearts. That is why we practice meditation.

We have become extremely lazy and indulgent about our own problems. We have never stopped to look at ourselves to find out who we are or what is happening in our ordinary life situation. Although we are extraordinarily interested in hearing some word of wisdom, if it is slanted toward personal demand we shy away from it. That is not to say that every one of us needs to be converted into some particular faith, but every one of us needs to slow down and sit, just slow down and sit. That is not a religious message, particularly. That is not recommending membership in a particular club. But, how long can we go on this way? I am not talking in terms of submission, but I am talking about working on ourselves. How long can we go on being window-shoppers on the path of life, rather than making a real investment in our innate sanity?

We can't be professional dilettantes forever. At some point, this thing called death will happen to us. We can't be dilettantes at that point, saying, "Oh, this is interesting—I am dying! My parents have gone through this. Well, good-bye. Adios. Here I go to the next life." When we encounter sickness, we can't be dilettantes. We are stuck with our aches and pains, our stuffed nose, or our cancer. We can't say that life was a rehearsal, and we would like to move on to the real show. At some point we have to stop and actually work on ourselves. We need some experience of a breakthrough, a gap, or a space, where we can sit and experience ourselves, review our lives but also see through our preoccupations and projections and uplift ourselves.

Every one of us has opportunities to do this. There are possibilities all the time. And it is about time! It would be terrible to have regrets later on. Regret is a very intense emotion, particularly when you had a chance that you ignored. "Five years ago I had the chance to do something about my life." "Ten years ago I had the chance." "A few seconds ago I had a chance." In other words, life is in our own hands. It is up to us to work on it. We are with ourselves all the time. It is time. You are always available to yourself. We can always work on ourselves and do something about our life. This might sound to you like a grand-dad's advice to his grandchildren, but nevertheless I am saying this for your own good! It's the voice of experience and the voice of my heritage speaking.

We have talked about the various strategies that we employ to keep ourselves comfortably confused and to construct an ego or self that seems solid and secure. The first level of this construction, form, is the basic dualistic fixation of me and other. The second stage, feeling, is trying to feel out yourself and your world fully, to make sure you know who is for and against you. The third aspect, impulse, is continually jumping to conclusions, trying to stabilize the situation. The fourth aspect is concept, where you put everything into a pigeonhole. And the fifth stage is the general situation of consciousness, in which your ego can actually operate in a complete network, where every entertainment is provided. If the big entertainments run out of steam, we produce little entertainments, which are known as subconscious gossip. Hopefully, everything is covered and everything's hunky-dory. We think that nothing can go wrong.

But there are always maintenance problems, not having enough entertaining subconscious gossip to occupy ourselves or enough larger-scale entertainment to fulfill our wishes. We have to find many babysitters to keep us occupied. You might find babysitters for three or four hours a day, but can you get a babysitter for twenty-four hours a day, seven days a week? Who's going to provide that level of entertainment for you all the time? That is an infantile, very soft approach. We might present ourselves as macho and try to look tough and self-reliant. We act as though we know how to deal with our business; we know how to deal with our boss, our subordinates, or our lovers. But if we haven't made friends with ourselves, it is a complete pretense. Actually, we are infantile, rather weak, soft, and pathetic.

On the other hand, this is not to say that the practice of

meditation will make you macho, the real macho warrior, at all. The point is to grow up rather than becoming a bandita or bandito. The technique of meditation is part of the process that undoes or dismantles our egotism very simply.

With the practice of meditation, to begin with, it is important to cut through the outskirts of the security ring of ego's scheme, as we talked about in the chapter on working with the fringe of the emotions. If you want to defeat a political regime, it is much wiser not to make the leader your enemy to begin with, but to work with his henchmen first. Similarly, we don't immediately try to intercept the basic fundamental bewilderment that is the core obstacle. That would be completely impractical. It's much better to work with situations on the fringe, which is working with the subconscious mind and all kinds of superficial neurosis that we generate. Simply work with the fringe, as we've already discussed, rather than trying to be too ambitious at the beginning. We have fantasies and realities. So go beyond fantasy and reach reality.

We can't play Cowboys and Indians in the name of meditation at this point. You need to pay more heed in the sitting practice of meditation, as much as you can. It is important to practice in the basic tradition of mindfulness. Without the mindfulness practice of peaceful living, other techniques or approaches that you apply are quite liable to create further pollution in this country. So, please be careful.

Having penetrated the outer ring of ego's fortress, how do we actually work with the fundamental dualistic fixation or basic bewilderment? There's no easy answer to that, no easy way to deal with that situation. But I would say that the best way to begin is by seeing through all kinds of self-deception in our life. This is done in the everyday practice of mindfulness in action.

We can observe the style and intentions of our everyday life situations: the way we brew tea or cook an egg, the way we walk down the street. This is not watching with an intensely critical attitude, trying to catch ourselves before we do something wrong. This watching is based on unconditional mindfulness, which is seeing things as they are, very precisely. That is the way to cut through our deceptions.

This may seem a little vague, and you might question how you can know if you're actually watching yourself correctly or whether you're deceiving yourself. The truth of the matter is that there's no telling. There's absolutely no telling. There's no list of dos and don'ts. You may make a list of things to accept and things to avoid, but if you do something with the wrong attitude, a do can become a don't. It's all based on ourselves, our personal attitude and the details of how we actually conduct ourselves. If you load the dishwasher very precisely but with intense aggression or irritation, is that a do or a don't? It's all up to you. Having that kind of somewhat unclear, relative reference point makes things much more interesting and instructive. From this point of view, you can't just rely on what's written in a book, whether it's this book or the Bible, the Buddhist Canon, the Koran, or some self-help literature. We actually have to pull up our own socks and be much more individually aware. In terms of developing mindfulness and awareness, you don't have the absolute security of inviolable dietary laws, spiritual commandments, or any other laws of behavior patterns to fall back on, particularly. You simply have to work with your basic sanity. That's asking a lot, but it can be done.

Purely working on the mindfulness-in-action situation alone is also not enough without the formal practice of meditation. This may seem somewhat doctrinaire or arbitrary, but I have found that it's the case. When the practice of meditation has a footing in your life and becomes a regular practice, a regular discipline, the contrast between sanity and neurosis in daily life becomes clear and precise. So working with both the formal practice of meditation and the post-meditation practice seems to be the only way to dismantle the fundamental core of ego's game. One of the main things that I would like to encourage is our confidence that we can actually do this ourselves. We can't simply rely upon prescriptions. But the one prescription, the one choiceless choice, is the need for the sitting practice of meditation. That is essential, absolutely. Without that, we don't slow down. Without that, we might be wholeheartedly interested, but we will theorize and drive ourselves nuts.

Basically, nobody can help the world without individual, personal discipline. However, when hundreds of individuals personally commit themselves to developing themselves through the practice of meditation, then, when they're all put together, it makes an orchestra of group sanity. As well, when we develop gentleness and softness through the process of sitting practice, it provides a kind attitude toward other individuals, not just toward ourselves. So some form of comradeship develops through sitting practice. Working together with each other, we begin to develop a mutual understanding of our confusion, our neurosis, the ache in our back, or the pain of our stiff neck. When we sit together, we develop mutual appreciation and mutual concern for one another.

Individuals begin to contribute their little portion of sanity to the bigger situation. Your contribution might be just a drop of sanity, but if everybody contributes, there will be lots of drops in the ocean. And it helps. From developing personal warmth toward ourselves we generate warmth and kindness to others in turn.

There are pitfalls to the group approach. Belonging to certain organizations, becoming members of the distinguished blah, blah, blah, saying that you're the student of the greatest blah blah, blah or that you're a scholar of the great blah, blah, blah doesn't seem to go along with shedding the arrogance of a bloated ego. So becoming a practitioner of meditation is different than self-promotion or encouraging group neurosis.

Having established genuine friendship, camaraderie, and fellowship with our fellow meditators, we still might be looking for credentials and security. We may wake up one morning feeling that we belong to a big meditators' world, a big syndicate or corporation of people who practice. However, when you get dressed, turn on the stove to cook your breakfast, and check your daily schedule, you find that you are alone, nevertheless. Trying to establish credentials based on belonging to a group shouldn't occur if you are working diligently on your own discipline. So if you look into the level of details, there's no problem. Without that, there are possibilities of cranking up self-deception.

We are also not talking here in terms of meditative discipline as a revolutionary act, regarding our meditation group as a little fortress from which we can launch our guerrilla warfare movement to change society. But we *are* talking about infiltration. Such infiltration can only begin with ourselves. We have to let meditative awareness infiltrate our being. In that way we can develop genuine comradeship with other practitioners.

Being together with each other, we are creating a society of its own particular type, an unconditional society, we might say. We don't necessarily all subscribe to the same political theories, sociological concepts, or religious ideas. The solidarity comes from our mutual understanding of mind, which comes from sitting together. Whether you are in a different physical location from other meditators doesn't matter. We feel some connection with others who also plop themselves down to sit every day. That sense of working together is not particularly heroic or exclusive—we don't condemn the non-sitters.

We have to work with ourselves first, so that we do not become a nuisance. So we work on our own discipline and life to begin with, so that we might exemplify the practice of meditation and mindfulness in action. That is how a meditative or mindful society, a genuine meditative tradition, could develop free from concept.

Mindfulness is an ancient approach, centuries old, millennia old. The practice of meditation and the discovery of fundamental mindfulness and awareness have arisen in many different cultures at many different times. The strength of the tradition relies on giving up every credential, every minute. There must be hundreds of thousands of people who have endeavored to give up their credentials throughout the world over all those years. Without their efforts we wouldn't have anything at all: no teaching, no discipline of meditation, nothing to work with. They didn't just give up their credentials and vanish into space. They worked extremely hard to transmit their discovery of mindfulness to others. It's a fantastic story, a fantastic case history, so to speak, that people could transmit the truth over all that time, without promoting their personal glory. That should actually give us a lot of hope that we can do this, too. It's possible for us as well. Taking pride in our discipline, in the positive sense, is both powerful and necessary, in both the sitting practice itself as well as in our daily living situation.

Having this sense of a heritage or ancestry of mindfulness can burst both the big and small bubbles of our egotism. Over all this time, nobody has remained an egomaniac. Not only that, but a lot of those people were able to powerfully manifest their basic sanity. This discipline of mindfulness and awareness becomes more powerful with each generation. As one of my ancestors said, the children will be much better than the parents, and the grandchildren will be much better than that. In the lineage of practitioners, mindfulness and the celebration of basic human sanity will never wane.

On the other hand, the whole thing is up to you. It's your personal experience. Through meditation we provide the room to be with ourselves. We also develop fellowship and mutual interest in our sisters and brothers in practice. Finally, we develop a feeling of surrendering and opening, to ourselves and to the world. We should take pride in this practice. Without arrogance, we should take pride in belonging to the vast family of all those who practice and live mindfully.

Editor's Afterword

The idea for this book first arose in 2009, when I began to connect with more and more people who were interested in mindfulness, meditation, and the insights they offer but were not seeking an affiliation with a particular path, teacher, or organization. Some of these were people facing serious life challenges who realized that meditation was helpful in working through these issues in their lives. For example, I met a lawyer who was working with prisoners in Guantanamo and was crumbling under the stress. I talked with people who were dealing with serious physical and mental illness, personally or in their families, as well as people affected by poverty, homelessness, and loss. I also met a number of people who didn't have such extreme challenges but simply wanted to meditate as a way to help themselves deal better with stress in their lives or as a means to develop greater appreciation and creativity.

I have been archiving and editing the work of Chögyam Trungpa for thirty-some years, having been his student since 1971. Over the years I've also presented his work in seminars and workshops, and it was in this context that I started to encounter so many people committed to meditation but not affiliated with any particular spiritual or religious tradition. It occurred to me that there was a great deal of unpublished material on meditation, mindfulness, and awareness in early seminars taught by Chögyam Trungpa and that this material might make a helpful book on the topic of mindfulness. I spoke about the project with Chögyam Trungpa's widow, Diana Mukpo, who is responsible for his literary estate. She agreed that it would be a valuable undertaking. We approached Shambhala Publications, who eagerly came on board, and I began work on the book in 2011.

In late September 2011, as background research for the book I attended a conference in New York City, *Creating a Mindful Society*, which was cosponsored by the Center for Mindfulness, the Omega Institute for Holistic Studies, and *Mindful* magazine. There I met a number of leaders of the mindfulness movement and several hundred very impressive teachers and practitioners of mindfulness in myriad walks of life. There was unbelievable energy and dedication in this group, and it felt that a community was coming together, forming around a shared commitment to bring mindfulness and awareness to bear on the challenges that we all face in our work and in our lives in general. I felt privileged to have stumbled into the midst of this vibrant "happening," and it encouraged me to move ahead with this project.

Chögyam Trungpa was himself deeply committed to mindfulness and awareness as the tools and the discipline that would be helpful to the thousands of people to whom he lectured and presented meditation in the 1970s and '80s. In virtually every seminar or public talk he gave in North America he encouraged people to meditate. I have helped to archive more than 2,500 of his talks, and I would estimate that meditation figured in about 2,450 of them.

From his earliest days in the West, he saw meditation as a

nonsectarian discipline that could benefit anyone and that anyone could practice. The instinct to emphasize meditation was there from the beginning of his time in the West. When he started his first center in the West in 1967 in Scotland, he wanted to call it the Samye-Ling Buddhist Meditation Center.

He went on to create a large network of Buddhist meditation centers in North America. Beginning in the 1970s, Chögyam Trungpa also started many nonsectarian institutions, including Naropa University, and he started a program of secular meditation called Shambhala Training, which is still being presented today.

I think he would have welcomed and been delighted by the growth of mindfulness in the United States and its application in so many fields, as represented preeminently by the work of Jon Kabat-Zinn, Sharon Salzberg, and Jack Kornfield, and by so many others.

In order to find the best material for this book, I searched through hundreds of transcripts of early talks given by Chögyam Trungpa in the 1970s. Most of these were available only as typewritten or handwritten transcripts. I made PDFs of the original often-faded transcripts and began to pore over them and listen to the audio recordings associated with them. At first I was challenged by much of the material. I realized that in order to do justice to these teachings on meditation and mindfulness, I was going to have to slow down and actually contemplate the material on an experiential level. I was going to have to take my own journey of mindfulness. Who would have guessed? This was painfully underlined for me when I "rushed" into one work retreat in an isolated house in the country, only to discover that I hadn't brought the right cord for my computer and that the printer cartridge I had brought with me didn't fit the printer in my retreat house. Embarrassed by my mindlessness, I had to drive several hours back to town and start over.

In the end, I was glad that the material didn't offer itself up to me easily. The more I practiced, relaxed, and let go, the more

I started to discover the jewels that were hidden in my files of old transcripts, and the more I started to appreciate the practice of meditation itself. I felt that I was reconnecting with an old friend, but that we were making a new relationship. Indeed, it seemed that it was all about making friends with oneself.

Even though he died more than twenty-seven years ago, Chögyam Trungpa's descriptions of the challenges and dilemmas of modern life are, to my ear and mind, still incredibly apt and telling for the twenty-first century. Perhaps because he came from such a different, a medieval, culture—Tibet in the 1950s—he was able to see certain aspects of Western life in very vivid relief or in contrast to his upbringing. This was also because he was such an inquisitive person. He was open to and interested in the people and the situations that he encountered in the Western world. Of course, he saw and spoke about great problems in our society, including materialism, speed, aggression, and fear, but he also was very attracted to and appreciative of Western culture. His use of the American idiom and his perceptive examples from our daily lives are part of what I think lends such a quality of aliveness to his presentations. His insights were often eerily prophetic, in that he looked deeply into his experience and what he saw happening in the world around him and projected the major themes and conflicts that would arise decades in the future. Most of the time, he was spot on.

A unique aspect of the meditation technique that Chögyam Trungpa presented was the emphasis he placed on paying more attention to the outbreath. He didn't invent this approach; it is described in the Tibetan tradition as mixing mind and breath, or as mixing mind and space. However, I think he was the first person to emphasize this as the basic technique for the whole sitting practice of meditation.

When I was putting together this manuscript, it struck me that the material I had chosen goes into far greater depth on the topic of the breath, and the outbreath in particular, than earlier books by Chögyam Trungpa. Indeed, the book shares much of the depth and the breadth of the practice instructions that he gave directly to his students, which had not been a prominent part of his previous books for a general audience. *Mindfulness in Action: Making Friends with Yourself through Meditation and Everyday Awareness* might be described as a contemplative discussion, in the sense of mixing meditative insight with a contemplation of everyday occurrences. This approach is true of much of Chögyam Trungpa's work, and it is particularly prominent here. He was always thinking about how people would actually apply the instructions he was giving, and how they could understand them in terms of their basic, ordinary lives. At the same time, he could evoke the atmosphere of deep practice in just a few words. Combining both, he opens our eyes to dimensions of life that we rarely examine in such depth.

In his instructions for meditation practice, Chögyam Trungpa always emphasized putting our attention on the outbreath as a means of connecting with our environment and dissolving, or stepping away from, an egocentric focus. Although he was passionate about this approach, he had tremendous respect for other techniques, among them vipassana meditation and Zen, particularly as taught by Shunryu Suzuki Roshi. He was appreciative as well of other contemplative traditions, such as the Christian contemplative approach of Thomas Merton and others. While his meditation instructions are distinct, they are compatible and quite complementary to many other techniques. At the same time, through the emphasis on the outbreath he offers the practitioner a uniquely potent way to link formal meditation practice with meditation in action, also known as mindfulness in action, or our meditative and contemplative experience of everyday life.

Another theme in *Mindfulness in Action* is the discussion of a gap that allows us to make an unconditional connection with awareness. In his meditation instructions, Chögyam Trungpa emphasizes the fundamental experience of letting our attention dissolve at the end of the outbreath. This is the *go* in his "touch and go" meditation instruction.* It is more "let go" than going somewhere. He talks about how, in our daily lives, an unconditional recollection of awareness can bring us fully into the present. The emphasis on dissolving or disowning one's attention or focus also distinguishes Chögyam Trungpa's teachings on mindfulness from many other approaches.

Another unique aspect of his meditation instructions was his emphasis on boredom as a necessary and a positive part of one's experience in meditation. The emphasis on boredom seems timely. I was interested recently to read Evgeny Morozov's piece in *The New Yorker*, "Only Disconnect: Two Cheers for Boredom," in which he talks about an essay in praise of boredom written by Siegfried Kracauer in 1924.† Kracauer's was partly a response to the hustle and bustle in the modern city of that era, along with other new phenomena such as the distracting power of the cinema and the radio. Morozov tells us that Kracauer's remedy was "extraordinary, radical boredom," a prescription that seems very close to the state of "cool boredom" that Chögyam Trungpa describes in *Mindfulness in Action*. Morozov goes on to talk about the current challenges to our awareness posed by our modern devices and the myriad ways we stay connected to information but disconnected from ourselves. In response to the attraction of the distraction of ever-available information and entertainment, Morozov tells how he put a safe in his apartment with a built-in timer where he can lock away his smart phone and his Internet cable for long periods of time. Reading this, I thought that taking up meditation might be a dignified alternative, a way to step away from the addiction to and distraction of our devices.

Another recent reference to the positive power of boredom was in Inara Verzemnieks's "Life along the Hundredth Meridian" in a recent issue of *The New York Times Magazine*. Talking

---

* See chapter 16, "Touch and Go."

† *The New Yorker*, October 28, p. 33.

about the affirming aspects of living in the empty landscape of Nebraska, Sharon Moreland is quoted as saying, "I think there are a lot of creative people out here. Our kids would play with spark plugs, sticks in the ground. I think you have to have a certain amount of boredom to create. . . . People here create things from what is around them. The openness and the distance between people inspires possibility."* I cannot but think that Chögyam Trungpa would have seconded this insight.

Although in many respects the material in this book is very simple, it is not at all simplistic. The book presents instructions for the beginning meditator, but it also goes deeply into the complexities and nuances of our practice. Using the analogy of gardening, some of the early chapters in *Mindfulness in Action* are like an instruction booklet for someone whose interest in horticulture is limited to wanting to plant basil in their window box or tulip bulbs in their backyard. But inevitably, if you take the next step and gardening becomes a real avocation, if you stay with it for any length of time, you are going to find yourself interested in compost and soil, in seed catalogs and new varieties of flowers or vegetables, in the different tools you may use in gardening, and all the ways to deal with garden pests and diseases. In short, you become a gardener.

Similarly, if you start meditating, you may initially be looking for a simple technique to reduce stress or help you find peace in the midst of the chaos of your life. If you keep practicing and go deeper into your practice, you will have lots of new questions and interests. This book presents fairly simple ideas about how to start meditating and what happens when you do. It also considers what may happen if you actually become a meditator and begin to see mindfulness as an ongoing journey.

When people practice diligently over a period of time, they usually find that their practice changes or evolves. They might

---

* December 8, 2013 (www.nytimes.com/2013/12/08/magazine/life-along -the-100th-meridian.html).

see this as a problem, especially if they begin to loosen up or relax. They may think that they are straying from the technique. Chögyam Trungpa encourages us to have greater faith in our experience and to regard whatever arises as workable, as part of the meditator's path.

This is somewhat akin to the experience that many parents have when they are worried about a problem their child is manifesting. Then they discover that their child is not the first child ever to have done or said this particular thing and that they are not the first parents who have ever reacted by doing or saying something particular in response. It turns out that everyone says and does these things. What a relief!

When you experience wild mood swings, spacing out, or other unexpected challenges in your meditation, it is highly likely that you are not the first person to do so, and it's not particularly a problem. Chögyam Trungpa often spoke of problems being promises. There are many examples of this in the sitting practice of meditation. For example, what we may often see as a problem in our practice—finding that the most difficult emotional and mental stuff eventually rises to the surface in our meditation—is actually the way to fully process it. In other words, it's good news. We may think that to be good meditators we should empty our minds of thoughts, but this is actually not the point, especially when it involves suppression or avoidance. We are just putting off the hard work that we will eventually need to do.

Chögyam Trungpa's approach to meditation reflects a deep respect for Western psychology. A book of his talks on psychology was published posthumously as *The Sanity We Are Born With: A Buddhist Approach to Psychology*. However, he had concerns about some therapies being used to reinforce egotism or to enshrine emotionalism, as opposed to emotion.

Chögyam Trungpa emphasizes the discovery of egolessness as a positive outcome from the practice of mindfulness and meditation. He distinguishes two approaches to or definitions of ego: "The term *ego* can be used to describe egomania, which is self-indulgence and a style of self that is looking for security and survival, trying to establish the certainty of one's existence. That is the confused and aggressive part of ego, which is completely blind. However, there is also another view of ego as intelligence and being assertive in a positive sense. [W]e're not only talking about the negative side of ego."* By egolessness, a term that occurs occasionally in *Mindfulness in Action,* he means an open and engaged approach to our lives, one that is compassionate and concerned with others more than with protecting our own self-centeredness. Elsewhere he described the realization of egolessness as "authentic presence." The epitome of authentic presence would be someone like Nelson Mandela. Egolessness, or overcoming the hard core of our egocentric selves, is not a milquetoast or dysfunctional aspect of ourselves but an empowered and expansive presence.

Working with our emotions is discussed in *Mindfulness in Action* primarily in relationship to meditation practice. In the meditation instructions that are given in chapter 16, "Touch and Go," Chögyam Trungpa stresses the importance of acknowledging our emotional and intense mental states of mind, actually looking at these as they arise rather than trying to avoid the difficulties and embarrassments that are uncovered in our practice. At the same time, after we have looked at and experienced our emotional and mental upheavals, the instruction is to label even these powerful feelings "thinking." We label them and return to the breath.

This approach is designed not only to keep us from bottling things up but also to encourage us to process our feelings and let the dramas dissolve—not get stuck in them over and over again, seemingly forever. Sometimes we treat our deepest emotional issues like precious objects that we pack away in our mind's attic. We might bring them out occasionally to admire

---

* See page 66.

them or show them to someone else, but then we carefully wrap them up again and put them back in storage. What Chögyam Trungpa suggests here is that once we take something out we should keep it on the mantelpiece, admire it, and delve deeply into it. Then, rather than packing it back up, we may be able to let it go. In meditation, this begins by labeling it "thinking." We may be living for a long time with what we've uncovered. It's not a one-shot deal. But when we uncover our emotional conflicts or deeply disturbing memories and then disown them to return to the breath, we make a commitment not to hold on to our difficult emotional baggage forever, as a precious family heirloom. Whether they are brilliant, dull, stinky, or beautifully perfumed, our most conflicted and intense thoughts and feelings are now on display. It is an act of bravery to acknowledge what's there. Then, letting go, with no guarantee, requires a real leap of faith.

Chögyam Trungpa saw the emotions as having great promise in their raw or awakened state. He saw them as powerful energies in our lives, in both very destructive and very creative ways. He talks about both aspects in *Mindfulness in Action*.

While reviewing material for the book, I was excited to discover two talks he gave in 1971 that appear in this volume as "The Fringe of Our Emotions" and "The Heart of Emotion." At that time Chögyam Trungpa was in the very early stages of working on the development of a therapeutic community for people with mental illness. He developed a series of postures and specially constructed rooms, as part of a system of working with energies, called Maitri Space Awareness. Maitri is the Sanskrit word for "loving-kindness." The goal of the space awareness practice is to develop loving-kindness through discovering, experiencing, and accepting our inherent state of being, in both its neurotic and awakened manifestations. Today, at Naropa University, the maitri postures and the rooms are primarily used in the contemplative psychology program as a way for students to work on understanding styles of neurosis and wisdom. A number of other individuals and organizations also work with this approach to maitri. My interest in bringing up this topic here is to point out that, very early on, Chögyam Trungpa was seeking methodologies to work with and acknowledge the wisdom of our emotions as well as the problems they create for us.

In fact, Chögyam Trungpa was interested in a wide range of body-mind techniques and disciplines. In addition to Maitri Space Awareness he created a series of theater exercises called Mudra Space Awareness; he invented a system of elocution, to improve people's relationship to their speech; and he created a number of exercises as part of developing an appreciation for what he termed "dharma art," which is based on artistic sensibility and creativity without aggression. These are just a few of the unique disciplines that he introduced. These were "mindfulness-in-action" practices, not designed to be practiced during formal meditation. He also introduced a practice for raising energy to be done at the beginning or the end of one's meditation practice, and he encouraged many students to include a formal practice to develop empathy and compassion as part of their meditation sessions.

My point in bringing this topic up is, again, to point to the open and complementary nature of his view and his work. On the one hand, he was very orthodox and somewhat conservative in how he taught meditation. On the other hand, he himself was a great innovator and an inventor of sorts in the field of mind-body disciplines. He talks about this combination of spontaneity and discipline in chapter 13, aptly titled "Spontaneous Discipline."

Chögyam Trungpa talks in this book about a natural progression from mindfulness to awareness, or insight, and also about how compassion naturally arises as an outgrowth of our experiences of opening and letting go in meditation. He shows us how these things can unfold and evolve without struggle, both in our meditation practice and in the application of meditative insight in our lives. He illustrates very empirically how a *path* of meditation evolves in our practice. It is also the natural, self-existing quality of all this that I find particularly heartening and illuminating. He encourages us to gently uncover the intelligence and good heart that are an intrinsic part of our being.

Sometimes when these aspects of ourselves are trying to break through, or at least twinkle in our mind's eye, we may feel that something is going wrong. We may panic and try to cover it all up again, as is discussed in the third and final section of the book. I love the image in chapter 18, "The Sword in Your Heart," of a sword that is trying to emerge while we wrap mental bandages and newspapers around the heart, out of fear or misunderstanding. We so often reach points in our practice where we feel too exposed, so we try to manufacture some safe harbor or attractive alter ego for ourselves. In *Mindfulness in Action* Chögyam Trungpa encourages us not to buy in to our self-deception but still to love ourselves with all of our foibles—our "tricks and triggers," as he sometimes called them.

Another key message in this book is that no one else can do this work for you. You have to do it for yourself. Others can be an example and a guide, but they cannot magically zap us into wakefulness. So there is a quality of hard truth in this book—no punches pulled, but also no false promises made. I think that in the long run when each of us has to face the tough stuff in life—and we all have to face it, one way or another—we will feel grateful that someone told us the truth, with a big grin rather than a long face. The ability to celebrate the best and the worst of life is one of this book's greatest gifts.

The world is always changing. This we know, but it seems that the pace of change is accelerating exponentially in this era. Institutions, ideas, and ideologies that may have sustained us in the past are being altered so quickly and in such fundamental ways that they may be almost unrecognizable to us, if they're not swept away altogether. At this uncharted and uncertain time in our history, mindfulness makes a significant contribution by offering us a way to remain fully and deeply engaged with our world without any necessary or particular religious or ideological affiliation. Chögyam Trungpa has talked about appreciating the "spirit" of life, in the sense of life being spirited or energetic. He suggested that, unlike our normal preconceptions, the spiritual dimension of life can be an approach "where there is energy happening, there is something to work on, and things are dynamic and provocative. There are flashes of negative energy, flashes of positive energy, flashes of destruction, flashes of hatred and love. All of this is happening within a big perspective."*

In this sense, being fully connected with life through the practice of mindful awareness provides fuel and sustenance for our life's journey. It is a way to appreciate both simplicity and complexity and a means to be not overwhelmed by chaos but cheerfully appreciative in its midst.

Mindfulness is on the cutting edge these days. Some worry that by entering the mainstream of American society it will become a diluted version of the real thing or, worse, that a treasured heritage of wisdom will be damaged. This is possible, indeed, but it is equally possible that by entering the mainstream of American society, meditation and mindfulness will tilt the balance of sanity just slightly, so that this sanity can manifest as wisdom that can be a force for good in a much bigger world. In doing so, mindfulness may promote a fuller appreciation of wisdom and compassion of all dimensions and traditions.

All over the world, the enormous advances in brain science are helping many to see meditation as a discipline that can be scientifically verified as useful and therapeutic. These developments were still in a very embryonic state when Chögyam Trungpa was teaching in America in the 1970s and '80s. The marriage of science and meditation may help to dispel the view of meditative discipline as what Chögyam Trungpa called "love-

---

* Chögyam Trungpa, "The Sacred Society," in *Work, Sex, Money* (Boston: Shambhala Publications, 2011).

and-lighty." I think he would be delighted to see these gooey clouds swept from the sky. He approached meditation as pretty hard-core, that is, as a grounded, realistic approach based on an intellectually rigorous contemplation of things as they are, not as a sappy version of how we would like them to be. At the same time, he used the word *magic* to point to the indescribably forceful power and beauty of reality. He spoke often of the marriage of intellect and intuition as the recommended course. Let us hope that this union will remain an indivisible part of the practice of mindfulness in times to come.

Chögyam Trungpa didn't view meditation as just a valuable tool or a necessary discipline. I think that he truly loved the practice of meditation. At the months-long programs where he taught meditation and where many of his students practiced for days and weeks, you could feel a kind of cool warmth that pervaded the atmosphere after people practiced meditation intensively. The coolness was the cooling off of the heat of neurosis and speed; the warmth was the openness, intelligence, and full heart generated by the practice. And it seemed that he exemplified and amplified these qualities and made it possible for all of us to aspire to further diligence in the practice. I am immensely grateful to him for the example that he set, for the wisdom that he shared, and for the instructions that he gave, which are gentle and loving but also piercing and luminous.

During one of these extended practice periods, a three-month program of study and practice in 1978, he wrote several poems about meditation practice. He ended one poem with these two lines:

Let us practice!
Sitting is a jewel that ornaments our precious life.

To that, I can only add "Amen!"

—CAROLYN ROSE GIMIAN

Acknowledgments and Gratitudes

I thought to call these acknowledgments gratitudes because I am writing them on the American Thanksgiving Day in November 2013. I am in a retreat house near Tatamagouche, Nova Scotia, Canada, where I have worked on more than a dozen books over the last eighteen years. I am grateful to have this place to work, and I am grateful to Chögyam Trungpa for having introduced me to the practice of solitary retreat, which has been so essential to my being able to do this work at all. I do most of the compilation and editing of books here, in what I call semi-retreat or a work retreat. The older I get, the more I seem to need the solitude and relative isolation. Practice informs the work, and the space of retreat helps me to see the shape of a project as it evolves, also enabling me to find the pieces of the puzzle that will be the book.

The Shambhala Archives provided access to audio- and videotapes, as well as to transcripts, of much of the material in this book. I would like to thank everyone at the Archives for their cheerful accommodation and their dedication to preserving these important records, especially Gordon Kidd, Jeanne Riordan, Chris Levy, and Sandra Kipis.

I have benefited from a number of lectures, discussions, and books about mindfulness. I would like to thank a number of the people who have influenced my understanding of and appreciation for mindfulness. Some are acquaintances, some are friends, some are close to me, and some I have met only through their books or lectures. My thanks go out to my husband, James Gimian, the publisher of *Mindful* magazine; Barry Boyce, the editor-in-chief of *Mindful: Taking Time for What Matters;* Jon Kabat-Zinn and Saki F. Santorelli of the Center for Mindfulness in Medicine, Health Care, and Society (Kabat-Zinn's book *Full Catastrophe Living* was an especially important resource); Sharon Salzberg, whose book *Real Happiness: The Power of Meditation—A 28-Day Program,* was an eye opener in the best sense of the word; Mirabai Bush, for many insights, references, great stories, much wisdom, and for her friendship; Jack Kornfield, for books, lectures, and exchanges over the years; Pema Chödrön, who gave me several wonderful opportunities to present meditation at her Smile at Fear programs, where I met people who fundamentally changed my worldview; a raft of presenters at the Creating a Mindful Society conference in New York, including Jon Kabat-Zinn, Saki Santorelli, Richard Davison, Janice Maturano, Congressman Tim Ryan, Ali and Atman Smith, Rhonda McGee, and Liz Stanley; Judith Lief, for her masterful editing of *The Path of Individual Liberation,* by Chögyam Trungpa—an important reference for this project—and for friendship and general merriment; Trudy Goodman, for insights gained over coffee in Paris, and for other conversations; and Melvin McLeod, who gave me opportunities to edit earlier versions of several chapters in this book for publication in the *Shambhala Sun* magazine.

Thanks are also offered to Robert Walker, who opened my eyes to much of the material on the foundations of mindfulness by Chögyam Trungpa, and to Andrew Safer, who has shared many resources and invited me to teach from the material in this book at the Family Life Center in St. John's, Newfoundland. Thanks also to Sister Loretta Walsh at the Family Life Center for accommodating and welcoming us; and thanks to all the workshop participants; and to Trudee Klautky, for generous sharing on many levels. Thanks also to Sherab Chödzin, the editor of *The Path Is the Goal: A Basic Handbook of Buddhist Meditation,* by Chögyam Trungpa, another important reference, and to Jenny Gimian, one of the most wakeful people I know.

I would like to thank Shambhala Publications and its founders, Sam and Hazel Bercholz, for supporting this project, and offer thanks to others at Shambhala, especially Sara Bercholz, my editor, and Nikko Odiseos, publisher, as well as Ben Gleason.

In most cases I do not know who transcribed the talks that have made their way into this book, but I am immeasurably grateful for these transcribers' efforts in the 1970s and '80s. Thanks to Barbara Blouin for correcting the transcripts of several talks I reviewed. Also, much gratitude to the students who made up the original audiences for these talks and asked such penetrating questions.

I am grateful for the support from Chögyam Trungpa's family, especially Diana J. Mukpo and Sakyong Mipham Rinpoche.

I am especially grateful to Chögyam Trungpa, whose teachings make my life worthwhile.

Finally, I am grateful to all practitioners of mindfulness, who help to bring gentle sanity into this troubled world.

CAROLYN ROSE GIMIAN
November 28, 2013

Sources

The material in *Mindfulness in Action* has been compiled from multiple sources and has been edited, condensed, and shaped for this book. Ninety percent of the material has not been published in any form before now. In some cases, where multiple sources are listed, only a few paragraphs of a source have been included in a particular chapter. In other chapters with more than one source, two or more sources have been extensively interwoven. The primary source is always listed first. Throughout the book, virtually all Sanskrit and Tibetan terms have been replaced by English equivalents. In several places, Chögyam Trungpa refers to specific phrases or teachings from some of the great Tibetan teachers in his tradition. I have noted these references below.

Chapter 1. Meditation: An Intimate Relationship with Ourselves

Chögyam Trungpa, "Meditation," in *Glimpses of Abhidharma: From a Seminar on Buddhist Psychology* (Boston: Shambhala Publications, 2011).

"Meditation: The Way of the Buddha" (Naropa University, Boulder, Colorado, June, 1974), transcript, Talks 1 and 2.

Chapter 2. Discovering Our Capacity to Love

"The Heart of Meditation" (Vancouver, British Columbia, September 28, 1979), transcript, Talk 1.

Chapter 3. How to Meditate

Some details of the meditation practice given here are based on oral instructions provided by Chögyam Trungpa to his students in talks and informal discussions over a number of years.

"The Heart of Meditation" (Vancouver, British Columbia, September 29, 1979), transcript, Talk 2.

"Dathun Letter" (Rocky Mountain Dharma Center [now Shambhala Meditation Center], Red Feather Lakes, Colorado, dates unknown). This is a manuscript based on instructions given at the Vajradhatu Seminaries and at the month-long dathun meditation practice. (*Dathun* is Tibetan for "month session.")

"Meditation Instructors' Training Seminars" (Karme-Chöling Retreat Center, Barnet, Vermont, December 1974), edited sourcebook, Talk 2, p. 5.

Chapter 4. The Teddy Bear of Breath

"Meditation Instructors' Training Seminars" (Karme-Chöling Retreat Center, Barnet, Vermont, December 1974), edited sourcebook, Talk 2. Note: The 25 percent emphasis on the breathing instruction comes from the Tibetan teacher Gampopa.

Chapter 5. Cool Boredom

"The Discovery of Egolessness" (New York City, March 1976), transcript, Talk 3.

Chapter 6. *Gentleness*

"The Heart of Meditation" (Vancouver, British Columbia, September 30, 1979), transcript, Talk 3.

Chapter 7. *Rhinoceros and Parrot*

"Dhyana and Samadhi" (Berkeley, California, March 2, 1974), transcript, Talk 2.

"Meditation: The Way of the Buddha" (Naropa University, Boulder, Colorado, June 1974), transcript, Talks 1 and 2.

Chapter 8. *The Present Moment*

"The Heart of Meditation" (Vancouver, British Columbia, October 1, 1979), transcript, Talk 4.

Chapter 9. *The Bridge of Compassion*

"Meditation Seminar" (Estes Park, Colorado, December 6, 1971), transcript, Talk 3.

Chapters 10–15

These chapters are based on transcripts of the seminar "Training the Mind" (Rocky Mountain Dharma Center, Red Feather Lakes, Colorado, August 18 to 24, 1974), transcripts, Talks 1 to 6. The Rocky Mountain Dharma Center is now the Shambhala Meditation Center. Note: In chapter 11, Marpa the Translator is the teacher who spoke about meditation as "trying to look at your own eyes without using a mirror."

Chapter 16. *Touch and Go*

"Dathun Letter." See source note at chapter 3.

Chapter 17. *Meditation and the Fourth Moment*

"The Tibetan Buddhist Path" (Naropa University, Boulder, Colorado, July 5, 1974), transcript, Talk 11. A version of this talk appeared as "Beyond Present, Past, and Future Is the Fourth Moment," *Shambhala Sun,* March 2006.

Chapter 18. The Sword in Your Heart

"The Discovery of Egolessness" (New York City, March 1976), transcript, Talk 1.

Chapter 19. Galaxies of Stars, Grains of Sand

"The Discovery of Egolessness" (New York City, March 1976), transcript, Talk 2.

"Meditation: The Way of the Buddha" (Naropa University, Boulder, Colorado, June 1974), transcript, Talk 3.

"The Tibetan Buddhist Path" (Naropa University, Boulder, Colorado, June 19, 1974), transcript, Talk 4.

Chapter 20. The Fringe of Our Emotions

"Understanding the Neurotic Aspects of Mind" (New York City, October 23, 1971), transcript, Talk 3.

Chapter 21. The Heart of Emotion

"Understanding the Neurotic Aspects of Mind" (New York City, October 24, 1971), transcript, Talk 4.

Gampopa is referenced in the original talk as the teacher who stated that the essence of the emotions is primordially awake. Naropa is referenced as the source of the analogy of the emotions freeing themselves to a snake unwinding itself in midair.

Chapter 22. A Mindful Society

"The Discovery of Egolessness" (New York City, March 1976), transcripts, Talks 4 and 5.

A Short Biography
of Chögyam Trungpa

Chögyam Trungpa was a pioneer in bringing mindfulness meditation and the teachings of Tibetan Buddhism to North America. He taught extensively in the United States and Canada from early 1970 until his death in 1987.

He was born in a remote area of Tibet in 1940, where he became the head of an important monastery and the governor of his district of Tibet. He was educated in the great meditative, scholarly, and contemplative traditions of Tibetan Buddhism. At the age of twenty, like many teachers from his generation, he left the country when the Communist Chinese took over the government. His journey to India, on foot, lasted more than ten months.

Even as a young man in Tibet, Chögyam Trungpa was quite drawn to the West, and after spending a few years in India, he was one of the first Tibetan teachers to travel to Europe. He studied for several years at Oxford University and then in 1967 established his first meditation center in Scotland. After an extensive study of English language, history, and philosophy at

Oxford, he became one of the earliest Asian teachers to present meditation and the Buddhist teachings in English in the West.

In early 1970, Chögyam Trungpa married and moved to North America. Here, he connected with thousands of students who were interested in meditation. He crisscrossed the continent giving public talks and weekend seminars in both the United States and Canada. His command of the English language and his understanding of the Western mind made him one of the most important influences on the development of Buddhism in the West. Within a few short years, he and his students established centers for the practice of meditation throughout major North American cities as well as rural retreat centers in Vermont and Colorado. Boulder, Colorado, and Halifax, Nova Scotia, became the headquarters for Chögyam Trungpa's work in North America. He also continued to travel and teach in Europe, where he established a European headquarters in Marburg, Germany, which later moved to Cologne.

In 1974 he joined with others to establish Naropa University, which for more than forty years has offered a contemplative approach to higher education, offering certificate and degree programs in meditation, psychology, Buddhism and other spiritual traditions, art, philosophy, and other subject areas. A number of the leaders in the mindfulness movement taught at Naropa, especially in the early years, including Sharon Salzberg, Jack Kornfield, Joseph Goldstein, Mirabai Bush, Mark Epstein, and Daniel Goleman.

In 1977, Chögyam Trungpa established Shambhala Training, a program to present meditation and the Shambhala tradition of warriorship to a broad audience. The author of more than two dozen popular books on meditation and Buddhism, he was an ecumenical teacher who sought out the wisdom in other schools of Buddhism and in other religions. He also studied and promoted a contemplative awareness of the visual arts, design, poetry, theater, and other aspects of Western art and culture.

In the last ten years of his life, Chögyam Trungpa taught extensively on the problems in society and the need to address them through the development of mindfulness and awareness. He also spoke extensively about creating an enlightened society, a theme that he was passionate about.

Many of his books on meditation, Buddhism, and the role of meditative awareness in everyday life are classics that are still widely read. Through the efforts of the editors he trained, new books continue to appear almost every year that draw on his lectures, which are among the principal holdings of the Shambhala Archives. *Mindfulness in Action: Making Friends with Yourself through Meditation and Everyday Awareness*—based on never-before-published archived materials—is the most recent such volume.

Index